HUNTING HITLER

HUNTING HITLER

New Scientific Evidence That Hitler Escaped Nazi Germany

By

Jerome R. Corsi, Ph.D.

Skyhorse Publishing

Skyhorse Publishing books may be purchased in bulk at special discounts for sales promotion, corporate gifts, fund-raising, or educational purposes. Special editions can also be created to specifications. For details, contact the Special Sales Department, Skyhorse Publishing, 307 West 36th Street, 11th Floor, New York, NY 10018 or info@skyhorsepublishing.com.

Skyhorse® and Skyhorse Publishing® are registered trademarks of Skyhorse Publishing, Inc.®, a Delaware corporation.

www.skyhorsepublishing.com

10 9 8 7 6 5 4 3 2 1

Library of Congress Cataloging-in-Publication Data is available on file.

ISBN: 978-1-62636-171-3

Printed in the United States of America

CONTENTS

Introduction

THE HUNT FOR HITLER CONTINUES

What really happened in the bunker during the last days of the war in Europe, while the Soviets were invading Berlin?

—Abel Basti, *Hitler's Escape* (2011)[1]

E veryone knows Adolf Hitler committed suicide by gunshot in his underground bunker on April 30, 1945.

As Russian troops neared the bunker's location in the Reich Chancellery in Berlin, fighting an urban battle street-by-street, Hitler preferred suicide to being captured and put on display as one of the most notorious mass murderers in history.

Everyone knows Hitler's death involved a double-suicide, as Eva Braun, his mistress

---

[1] Abel Basti, *El Exilio De Hitler: Las pruebas de la fuga del Führer a la Argentina* (Buenos Aires, Argentina: Sudamericana, 2012), p.19. Title in English: *Hitler's Escape: The Proof of Hitler's Escape to Argentina.*

and long-time female companion, married Hitler in a simple ceremony in the bunker before she too took her life by biting down on a cyanide capsule.

Seated on a couch in Hitler's private chambers in the underground bunker, Eva Braun died first, but she died as the bride of her beloved Fürher.

Their bodies were taken, as Hitler had commanded, outside the bunker and doused with gasoline to be cremated in a shallow trench dug for that purpose in the garden of the Reich Chancellery, right outside the secret entrance to the bunker below.

The Russian army, in liberating Berlin, came across the bodies of Hitler and Eva Braun; hurriedly, the Russian army buried the charred remains in a secret location in Berlin, keeping the bodies safe until the cessation of hostilities permitted their safe transport to Moscow.

Who would dare be silly enough to think Hitler escaped Berlin to run away to a safe haven such as Argentina?

Anyone who questions that Hitler died by suicide in his bunker in the closing hours of World War II in Europe is by definition considered a "conspiracy theorist"—a polite way of claiming the doubter is a proverbial nut-case.

But in recent years, the world has come to see that the scientific proof offered for decades by the Russians to back this politically correct version of Hitler's demise is deeply flawed.

Moreover, the cover-up story, concocted and published in 1947 by Hugh Redwald Trevor-Roper, then a British 32-year-old history graduate student who had worked during World War II as a British military intelligence officer, turned out to be inconsistent in several major aspects of the story with other arguably authoritative accounts of Hitler's demise.

The hunt for Hitler continues

The research and analysis presented here will make a scientific case that no proof exists or has ever existed that Hitler died in Berlin as recounted in Trevor-Roper's official version of events.

Examining the now-declassified FBI and US military intelligence files, a compelling case can be made that US investigators suspected from the beginning that Hitler had escaped, but were willing to go along with the Trevor-Roper story for political reasons.

The point of this book is that hunting Hitler must continue until the weight of scientific evidence proves one way or the other whether Hitler died by suicide in the bunker on April 30, 1945, or if he escaped, to die elsewhere.

Hunting Hitler, the world's most notorious mass murderer, an international criminal whose crimes against humanity and the law of nations have never been adjudicated, must continue until we know the truth.

History should not rest until the Hitler chapter is closed, not with politically convenient lies, but with the truth.

With the truth in hand, steps can be taken to adjudicate blame, not just for the unspeakably horrendous crimes Hitler committed, but also for the inexcusable crimes committed by those who helped Hitler escape.

Just exactly how did Hitler die?

The major problem with the story that Hitler and his mistress committed suicide is that it doesn't hold up under a few pointed questions:

- "What? Did Hitler take a cyanide capsule or did he shoot himself?" the skeptic asks. "Or did he do both, biting down on the glass capsule containing the cyanide and then shooting himself in the head second, to make sure he killed himself one way or another?"

- "How about Eva Braun? Did she shoot herself, or did Hitler accept the gentleman's responsibility by shooting her to spare her the indelicate task of ending her own life with a bullet to the head?"

- "Where was Eva Braun sitting when she died, to Hitler's right or left? If she was sitting on Hitler's left, did Hitler shoot her in the right temple? Or the left temple, if she was sitting on Hitler's right?"

- "Or did Hitler just watch Eva take her cyanide capsule, waiting to make sure she was dead, before he killed himself?"

- "Where did Hitler shoot himself? In the center of his forehead, or was that too awkward for holding the pistol and squeezing the trigger? Or did Hitler simply put the pistol in his mouth to blow his brains out through the back of his head? If the latter, how did he pull the trigger? With one thumb or two thumbs?"

- "Or if Hitler shot himself in the temple, did he shoot himself in the right temple or the left temple? Shooting himself in the center of the forehead was equally problematic to shooting himself in the mouth. How did Hitler steady the pistol against his forehead, especially if he used both thumbs to pull the trigger?"

- "If Hitler had Parkinson's disease, how did he steady his hands enough to be sure he didn't miss, either in shooting himself or in shooting Eva Braun?"

The truth, as we shall see in the next few chapters, is that we know nothing for certain regarding how Adolf Hitler and Eva Braun committed suicide. The official narrative has

Adolf Hitler shooting himself in the mouth after watching Eva Braun die of cyanide poising, but how did that narrative come to be established, especially since there is no physical evidence authenticating how either died?

Then, there are a score of questions about the immediate aftermath of the double-suicide. Did Hitler and Eva lock themselves away in one of the bunker's personal rooms to commit their final acts? If so, how did others in the bunker get in to recover their bodies (or to make sure that the suicide attempt hadn't somehow been botched)?

Who heard any shots that were fired, and how did those in the bunker gain entrance if the room had been locked by Hitler and Eva Braun to make sure they were not interrupted in the act of killing themselves?

How were Hitler and Eva's bodies discovered? Did eyewitnesses in the bunker immediately carry the bodies outside to be cremated, or did eyewitnesses in the bunker hold some sort of viewing or service for the newly wed and even more newly deceased Fürher and his bride?

As we shall see, the truth is that we have no authoritative account of the discovery and disposal of the bodies of Hitler and Eva Braun after committing suicide, as the several available accounts conflict on many important details.

Where are the photographs of the Fürher in death?

Truthfully, none of these questions can be answered beyond a reasonable doubt in part because no one actually saw Hitler pull the trigger or Eva Braun swallow the cyanide capsule. The bodies of Adolf Hitler and Eva Braun were never recovered or preserved for positive identification, and there are no photographs of Adolf Hitler and Eva Braun's joint suicide.

Within hours, the Russians rejected the one photograph supposedly showing Hitler in death as nothing more than one of Hitler's many doubles.

To all but the most gullible, the photo of Hitler with a bullet hole in the center of the forehead looks nearly as contrived as the tattered Hitler outfit stained by food droppings that the double is wearing at the time of death, to say nothing of the double's darned socks, and the fact that the double's corpse was measured at three inches shorter than Hitler.

Looking at the death of the Hitler double, we wonder if he knew this would be his ultimate fate? Who told him that now was the moment duty called for him to stand in for Hitler not at some silly parade or public event, but in the dissimulation of the Fürher's last moment—a moment the double was expected to live out to its last nasty shot good bye.

But then, what was the point of murdering a Hitler double if Adolf Hitler and Eva Braun actually did commit suicide? Why not just take some photographs of the real deal to prove to the world that Hitler and his mistress were dead, allowing the visual evidence to end the controversy over how they died?

As this book will demonstrate, the truth is that when the Russians entered Hitler's underground bunker in Berlin, Adolf Hitler and Eva Braun were gone. Neither were ever captured, and their bodies were never found.

When the Russians burst into the bunker, Hitler and Eva Braun were simply missing.

Exactly what happened to them has been a mystery since April 30, 1945, the date the two reportedly committed suicide.

Since that day, the whereabouts of Hitler and Eva Braun have remained a mystery, despite official protestations that they killed themselves and their bodies were burned before the Russians arrived at the Hitler bunker in the Reich Chancellery in Berlin.

The story of Hitler's marriage and suicide: an elaborate cover-up?

Certainly, the eyewitnesses to Hitler and Eva's suicides would have left authoritative accounts, maybe even signed affidavits attesting to the fact that they saw the Führer and his bride not only in their final moments of life, saying a tearful goodbye to the remaining few faithful yet with them in the bunker, but also in death.

But when we seek the eyewitness testimony, we find the personal accounts to be as disappointing as the one remaining photograph of the sad Hitler double with the bullet hole in the middle of his forehead, dead with his mouth open as if the body were in a long snore, or perhaps just gasping for his last breath.

The truth is that supposed eyewitness accounts to Hitler and Eva Braun's final hours conflict in many important details, leading to the inevitable conclusion that the eyewitnesses freely added fiction, sometimes masked as supposition or educated guesses, to fill in details where their memories were incomplete.

As we shall see, a close reading of the various supposedly authoritative accounts of Hitler's final days differ in many important aspects, including: Who was with Hitler in his final hours? What did Hitler say and do?

In the final analysis, a thoughtful reader begins asking whether the eyewitness accounts could have been entirely fabricated to cover up a truth no one at the time wanted to acknowledge. Could Hitler have escaped?

Are the discrepancies in the eyewitness accounts explainable because eyewitnesses told military intelligence officers what the officers wanted to hear? Or were the eyewitness accounts intended from the beginning to be artful lies to protect the Fürher who had escaped, taking with him the loyalty of the die-hards he left behind?

Where is the proof that Hitler didn't escape?

These are the questions I have been asking since I was a child, being born a year after the war in Europe ended and growing up in the 1950s.

Somehow, it seemed that if Hitler had died on April 30, 1945, the facts surrounding his death should have been easy to prove.

All too convenient was the explanation that the United States lacked the proof because the Soviets liberated Berlin and the Soviets absconded with Hitler's remains back to Moscow before the United States and its allies, including the British and the French, had a chance to demand proof from the Soviets that Hitler was dead.

However, it now appears that not only did Stalin and the Russians doubt Hitler was dead, but that those doubts were also shared by General Dwight D. Eisenhower, who was at that time the Supreme Commander of the Allied Forces who won World War II.

If both Stalin and Eisenhower had doubts about Hitler's demise, then how did the double-suicide story become the official narrative? And to such an extent that to dispute whether Hitler might have escaped was a question no serious or mature adult would dare ask in public?

I decided to write this book when international news broke that credible DNA testing proved the skull the Russians had claimed was Hitler's since the end of World War II was actually that of a 40-year-old woman.

The story of that DNA testing is where the first chapter of this book begins.

1 | SCIENTIFIC PROOF HITLER ESCAPED GERMANY

A skull long believed to be that of Adolf Hitler actually belonged to a woman, according to an American scientist who has taken DNA samples from it.

—Sky News, "Where in the World is Hitler's Skull?" Sept. 28, 2009 [2]

In February 1945, Secretary of State James F. Byrnes accompanied President Franklin D. Roosevelt to a meeting with Winston Churchill and Joseph Stalin in Yalta, a city in Crimea (southern Ukraine). During a casual moment at the meeting, Byrnes asked Stalin whether he believed Hitler actually died in Berlin at the end of World War II. In his 1947 book,

---

[2] "Where in the World is Hitler's Skull?" Sky News, Sept. 28, 2009, http://www.foxnews.com/story/2009/09/28/where-in-world-is-hitler-skull/.

Speaking Frankly, Byrnes recounted the conversation: "I asked the Generalissimo [Stalin] his views of how Hitler died. To my surprise, he said he believed that Hitler was alive and that it was possible he was then either in Spain or Argentina."[3] Some ten days later, Byrnes asked Stalin if he had changed his views, and Stalin said he had not. Stalin retained the same beliefs until the end of his life.

In May 1945, shortly after the death of President Franklin D. Roosevelt, Harry Hopkins, one of FDR's closest advisors, undertook a special mission to Moscow at the request of President Harry Truman to prepare for the upcoming conference with Churchill and Stalin, scheduled to begin in July 1945 in Potsdam, Germany. In a discussion with Stalin in Moscow, Hopkins commented that he hoped Hitler's body, which had not yet been recovered, would be found by the Russians. Stalin replied that Soviet doctors thought they had identified the body of Joseph Goebbels, Hitler's minister of propaganda; and of Erich Kempka, Hitler's chauffeur; but that he personally doubted that Goebbels was dead. He said the whole matter was strange, and that the various talks of funerals and burials struck him as being very dubious. He further explained that he thought Hitler, Goebbels, and General Hans Krebs, the chief of staff of the German army, along with Hitler's secretary Martin Bormann, had all escaped and were in hiding. Hopkins commented that the Nazis had several large submarines, and he was aware no trace of Hitler had yet been discovered. Stalin responded that the Germans were using those submarines to transport gold and negotiable assets to Japan, with the connivance of Switzerland. He further

---

3   James F. Byrnes, *Speaking Frankly* (New York: Harper & Brothers, 1947), page 68.

mentioned that his intelligence service was investigating these Nazi submarines, but Russia had also failed to find any trace of Hitler. In concluding the discussion, Stalin speculated that Hitler and the other top Nazis he mentioned may have fled to Japan.[4]

Yet as early as May 4, 1945, Russian army troops claimed to have found the bodies of Adolf Hitler and Eva Braun buried outside the Führerbunker in the garden of the Reich Chancellery in Berlin. Why was Stalin yet skeptical that Hitler had died in Berlin, when his troops had discovered what appeared to be incontrovertible proof that Adolf Hitler and Eva Braun had died in the bunker? Shrouded in uncertainty is exactly how the mystery of Hitler's last days began.

The Russian army at the Führerbunker, May 1945

The first Russian troops reached the Reich Chancellery on May 2, 1945. A book published in New York in 1968 by Lev Bezymenski, a Russian military intelligence officer who served on the staff of Russian General G. K. Zhukov in the battle of Berlin, entitled *The Death of Hitler: Unknown Documents from Soviet Archives,* caused a worldwide

---

[4] Memorandum by Assistant Secretary of State Charles E. Bohlen, "Memorandum of First Conversation at the Kremlin, 8 PM, Moscow, May 26, 1945," included in "The Hopkins Mission to Moscow," US Department of State, Foreign Relations of the United States, Diplomatic Papers, The Conference of Berlin (the Potsdam Conference), May 1945, pp. 21-62, archived at University of Wisconsin Library, http://digicoll.library.wisc.edu/cgi-bin/FRUS/FRUS-idx?type=div&did=FRUS.FRUS1945Berlinv01.i0011&isize=text and http://images.library.wisc.edu/FRUS/EFacs/1945Berlinv01/reference/frus.frus1945berlinv01.i0011.pdf.

sensation.[5] For the first time, the Soviet Union allowed access to documents from Moscow's secret archive, including both the records of the autopsy the Russians conducted on corpses they believed were the bodies of Adolf Hitler and Eva Braun, as well as the extensive files from "Operation Myth." Not accepting the autopsy results that indicated that the bodies the Russians found at the Reich Chancellery in Berlin were those of Hitler and Eva Braun, Stalin launched "Operation Myth" in December 1945 to conduct a comprehensive investigation of all possible witnesses to Hitler's last days in the Führerbunker. The Soviet investigation was labeled "Operation Myth" to reflect Stalin's conviction that Hitler had escaped Berlin.

Bezymenski disclosed that on the afternoon of May 2, 1945, Russian Lieutenant Colonel Ivan Isayevich Klimenko—commander of the Counter Intelligence Section of the 79th Rifle Corps of the Third Shock Army—received orders to inspect the Reich Chancellery that the Fifth Shock Army had stormed the night before. Once he received his orders, Klimenko jumped into a jeep and headed toward the Reich Chancellery, followed by a Russian army truck containing various German witnesses and soldiers who claimed under interrogation to have heard Hitler and Joseph Goebbels, the Reich Minister of Propaganda for Nazi Germany, commit suicide in the Chancellery. Bezymenski quotes Klimenko as follows:

> We drove up to the Chancellery, went into the garden, and arrived at the emergency exit of the Führerbunker. As we approached this exit, one of the Germans shouted: "That is Goebbels' corpse! That is the corpse of his wife!

---

5   Lev Bezymenski, *The Death of Adolf Hitler: Unknown Documents from Soviet Archives* (New York: Harcourt, Brace, & World, Inc., 1968).

I decided to take these corpses with us. Since we did not have a stretcher, we placed the corpses on an unhinged door, maneuvered them onto the truck (it was a covered vehicle), and returned to Plötzensee.

The day after, May 3, 1945, the corpses of six Goebbels children and the corpse of General Krebs were found in the bunker. They too were taken to Plötzensee.[6]

The six Goebbels children were found dead in their beds in the bunker, having been poisoned by their parents. The next day, German Vice-Admiral Hans-Erich Voss, one of the final occupants of the Führerbunker during the Battle of Berlin and a staff member of Hitler's appointed successor, Grand Admiral Karl Dönitz, made a positive identification of the Goebbels' bodies. Lieutenant-General Krebs was the chief of the general staff of the German army. He was identified by a strip of cloth bearing the name "Krebs," found in the lining of his uniform jacket near the left side pocket.

Having failed to find Hitler's body on May 2, 1945, Klimenko returned to the Reich Chancellery the next day with Voss. Here is how Klimenko described the decision to visit the Führerbunker a second time:

> Naturally we asked Voss where Hitler might be. Voss gave no clear answer and told us only that he had left Berlin together with Hitler's adjutant, who had told him that Hitler committed suicide and that his corpse had been burned in the Chancellery garden.[7]

---

[6]   Russian Lieutenant Colonel Ivan Isayevich Klimenko, quoted in Lev Bezymenski, op.cit., pp. 30-31. Parenthesis in original.

[7]   Ibid., p. 31.

Once at the Chancellery, Klimenko decided to look around.

> We arrived with the jeep carrying me, Voss, a Lieutenant Colonel of the [Russian] Army Counter Intelligence Service, and an interpreter. At the Chancellery, we went down into the bunker. It was dark. We illuminated our way with flashlights. Voss behaved somewhat strangely; he was nervous, mumbling unintelligibly. After that we climbed up again and found ourselves in the garden, not far from the emergency exit.
>
> It was close to 9 p.m. We stepped up to a big dried-up water tank for fire-fighting. It was filled with many corpses. Here Voss said, pointing to a corpse: "Oh, this is Hitler's body!"
>
> This corpse was dressed; the feet were in mended socks. After a moment Voss began to have his doubts: "No, no, I can't say with certainty that this is Hitler." Frankly, I also had my doubts because of the mended socks![8]

Deciding this was not Hitler's body, Klimenko and Voss left the corpse in the bunker where it was found. When Klimenko and Voss left, however, the body was rediscovered by a group of Russian soldiers who were convinced they had found Hitler's corpse. Taking the corpse outside the bunker, the Russian soldiers filmed the corpse, making sure the bullet hole in the middle of the forehead was clearly visible, and bragged to the press that Hitler's body had been found. The corpse bore a certain resemblance to Hitler but was quickly determined to be a Hitler double, as suggested by the fact that the corpse was wearing no shoes,

---

[8] Ibid., p. 32. Parenthesis added for clarity.

clearly showing darned socks; also, the uniform on the corpse was food-soiled, which was very uncharacteristic of the Führer, who was known for his fastidious nature and meticulous dress. Particularly damning was a height measurement that showed the doppelgänger to be three inches shorter than Hitler.

Still, the discovery of this Hitler double was misleading to the Russian investigation into the death of Hitler, as can be seen from Klimenko's continuing narrative:

> Then came May 4. From early morning the search among the prisoners for possible witnesses went on. Around 11 a.m. I returned to the garden of the Chancellery together with six witnesses. We ran to the water tank, but the corpse had already vanished![9]

Klimenko and his witnesses discovered the vanished corpse laid out in one of the many halls of the Chancellery. One of the six witnesses claimed the corpse might be Hitler, but the other five denied it categorically. It was at that point that Klimenko learned Russian soldiers had dug up two more corpses they believed might be Adolf Hitler and Eva Braun:

> Together with me were Platoon Leader Panassov and a few soldiers. One of my soldiers asked: "Where did you find the Goebbels?" We went back to the garden, to the bunker exit.
>
> Private Ivan Churakov climbed into a nearby crater that was strewn with burned paper. I noticed a bazooka in there and called to Churakov: "Climb out quickly, or you may be blown to bits!" Churakov

---

[9] Ibid.

answered: "Comrade Lieutenant Colonel, there are legs here!"

We started to dig them out and pulled two corpses from the crater: the bodies of a man and a woman. Of course at first I didn't even think that these might be the corpses of Hitler and Eva Braun, since I believed that Hitler's corpse was already in the Chancellery and only needed to be identified. I therefore ordered the corpses to be wrapped in blankets and reburied.[10]

The next day, Russian intelligence officers of the 79th SMERSH counter-intelligence unit learned from high-ranking prisoners that the bodies of Hitler and Eva Braun had been burned before being buried. So, reconsidering that the corpses might be Hitler and Eva Braun, Russian intelligence ordered the badly charred corpses to be dug up again and hauled away in ammunition crates. While one of the corpses was clearly male and the other female, the bodies were too badly burned to permit facial recognition. Still, after additional investigation, including an identification of the corpses by Harry Mengerhausen, one of Hitler's bodyguards, and what Bezymenski identified as a "forensic autopsy," the officers determined that these two corpses were Adolf Hitler and Eva Braun.

Playing on the use of "Ivan" as a generic reference to Russian soldiers (as well as the first name of the Russian soldier who supposedly found Hitler's corpse) Bezymenski bragged, "Ivan came to Berlin and found the corpse of War Criminal Number One."[11]

---

[10]   Ibid., p. 33.

[11]   Ibid., p. 34.

The Russian autopsy evidence

On May 5, 1945, according to secret Soviet documents serving as the source materials for Bezymenski's 1968 account, the corpses of Hitler and Eva Braun were transported from the center of Berlin to the northern suburb of Buch, where various divisions of the staff of the Russian Third Shock Army were stationed. "In place of the soldier Ivan, a new character comes to the fore—Dr. Faust Shkaravski," Bezymenski wrote. "I have not invented his first name: it is really the name of a man of advanced age, forensic physician by profession, who at the time was Chief Expert of Forensic Medicine with the 1st Byelorussian Front."[12] On May 8, 1945, coincidently "V-E Day," celebrating "Victory in Europe," Dr. Shkaravski directed a team of four additional qualified and competent Russian forensic pathologists in conducting an autopsy on the two corpses thought to be Hitler and Eva Braun. The autopsy was conducted in a pathology laboratory that had been converted from a clinic that had once served as a mental institution.

Given the disfiguration of the bodies, the autopsy doctors quickly determined that the teeth offered the best opportunity for a positive identification.

The autopsy reports published in Bezymenski's book indicated that, from the male corpse, the following dental specimens were handed over to the SMERSH Section of the Third Shock Army on May 8, 1945: a maxillary bridge of yellow metal, consisting of nine teeth from the upper jaw; and a burned lower jaw consisting of fifteen teeth. From the female corpse, the following teeth were recovered for identification purposes: a gold bridge of the lower jaw with four front teeth. On May 9, 1945, Vasili Ivanovich

---

[12] Ibid., p. 38.

Gorbushin, the deputy chief of counter-intelligence in the Third Shock Army, found and visited Hitler's dentist, a Dr. Bruck, and his dental assistant, Käthe Heusermann. As suggested by Heusermann, Gorbushin was able to find X-ray photographs of Hitler's teeth, along with detailed dental records and photographs of Hitler's teeth, plus a few gold crowns that had been prepared but never installed. Following Heusermann's instructions, Gorbushin found a dental technician named Fritz Echtmann, who had worked on Eva Braun.

As quoted by Bezymenski, Gorbushin reported the following:

> In answer to my questions, Käthe Heusermann and Fritz Echtmann described Hitler's teeth from memory in minute detail. Their information about bridges, crowns, and fillings corresponded precisely with the entries in the medical history and with the X-ray pictures that we had found. Next we asked them to identify the jawbones which had been taken from the male corpse. Frau Heusermann and Echtmann recognized them unequivocally as those of Adolf Hitler.
>
> In a similar procedure we next asked the dentists to describe Eva Braun's teeth. After they had both answered our questions exhaustively, we placed before them the gold bridge which had been taken from the mouth of the female corpse during the autopsy.
>
> Käthe Heusermann and Fritz Echtmann declared without hesitancy that this prosthesis belonged to Eva Braun. Fritz Echtmann added that the special construction of the bridge prepared for Eva Braun was his own invention and that so far no dental prosthetist had used a similar method of attachment.

Next, our medical experts met again. After examination of the medical history, X-ray pictures, and jawbone with the teeth of the charred male corpse which had been found on May 4 in the garden of the Chancellery, the experts came to the definite conclusion that these were Adolf Hitler's teeth.[13]

The presence of crushed glass ampules and traces of cyanide compounds found in the oral cavities of both bodies led the autopsy doctors to identify the cause of death for both the male and female corpses as poisoning via cyanide compounds. Curiously, the autopsy of the male corpse did not find evidence of a gunshot wound, although the autopsy doctors did note a piece of the cranium was missing. This finding was at odds with intelligence reports that Hitler had both shot himself and taken a cyanide capsule. Despite the findings that the cause of death for both corpses was cyanide poisoning, the Russian autopsy did not include a dissection of the internal organs of either corpse. Additionally, the autopsy of the female corpse indicated evidence of metal shrapnel fragments in the throat, which had caused bleeding in the throat, chest, and lungs. Yet there was no evidence that Eva Braun had been wounded by an artillery shell. Nor would wounds to a corpse be expected to cause bleeding. The type of hemorrhage observed in the female corpse could only have been sustained if the heart had been beating strongly enough to create pressure in the body's arteries and veins to force blood out. In other words, the female was alive at the time the shrapnel wounds were suffered. Bleeding would not result had the corpse been hit by shrapnel after committing suicide by ingesting cyanide compounds.

Curiously, the autopsy report published by Bezymenski indicated that the left testicle could not be found anywhere

---

[13]   Ibid., pp. 54-55.

in the body of the male corpse.[14] This rather sensational finding was likely highlighted in the Russian autopsy reports because the finding corresponded with popular rumors circulating about Hitler's supposed sexual dysfunction. Such evidence, however, could not be used to identify the corpse as Hitler's, because he had never permitted even his personal doctors to examine him so thoroughly. Somehow the Russian pathologists—evidently persuaded by the rumors that Hitler suffered this physical defect to his reproductive biology—believed that including the discussion of the missing testicle would somehow serve as final proof that the body had to be Hitler's.

Still, despite these problems and inconsistencies, the Russian forensic pathologists relying primarily on the dental evidence were convinced that the two corpses Russian soldier Ivan Churakov found buried in the garden of the Reich Chancellery were the bodies of Adolf Hitler and Eva Braun. Additionally persuasive to Soviet intelligence was the discovery of two German shepherds buried in the Reich Chancellery garden. The larger of the two dogs was found to have died by cyanide poisoning, but only after a capsule amulet had been forced into the dog's throat, with his jaws held open and the capsule broken open with pliers. The dog also appeared to have suffered fatal brain damage from a severe blow to the head. Why the dog had to be bludgeoned to death in addition to having been poisoned was not clear. Still, the Russian intelligence officers just assumed the larger dog was Hitler's favorite dog, "Blondi," who had been given a cyanide capsule to prove to Hitler that the poison pills worked.

"The circumstances of the death of Hitler, Goebbels, and others had been thoroughly examined by the medical

---

14   Ibid., page 49.

experts," Bezymenski concluded, noting that top officials in Moscow, including Field Marshall Zhukov and Joseph Stalin, were informed of the results in May 1945. Still, Stalin remained unconvinced that the forensic evidence from the autopsy proved Hitler was dead. In December 1945, Stalin ordered the initiation of "Operation Myth" to interview any and all witnesses of Hitler's last days who could be tracked down and found. What we will discover in the next chapter is that the eyewitness phase of "Operation Myth" raised more questions than it solved, if only because eyewitness testimony produced multiple and generally conflicting versions of Hitler and Eva Braun's last hours. In the concluding section of his 1968 book, Bezymenski was forced to acknowledge that the testimonial evidence obtained by the "Operation Myth" investigation was anything but conclusive. Still, Bezymenski leaves no doubt that the forensic evidence discovered by the medical pathologists at the laboratory was sufficient to convince him that the bodies belonged to Hitler and Eva Braun.

The strange journey of the Hitler and Eva Braun corpses

In 1992, award-winning Russian television journalist Ada Petrova approached Anatoli Prokopenko, then the director of the Russian "special archive" that housed the autopsy records, files from "Operation Myth," and Hitler's skull fragments. In 1992, the Russians were still enjoying the relative openness experienced in the Soviet Union under the leadership of Mikhail Gorbachev. Ruling Russia from 1985 to 1991 as general secretary of the Communist Party, Gorbachev had launched a dual program of *perestroika*, or "restructuring," and *glasnost*, or "openness," during which Russia relaxed state security in favor of instituting a policy of sharing information more openly than had been traditional under communist rule. Under *perestroika* and *glasnost*, foreign journalists were given access to state secrets and government archives with an openness that had been unimaginable under previous leaders like Stalin.

In discussions with Petrova, Prokopenko dropped the bombshell that Hitler's skull was "right here in Moscow." In 1993, Petrova and British journalist Peter Watson were given access to the special archive and were allowed to examine Hitler's skull fragments. They published their findings in London and New York in a 1995 book entitled *The Death of Hitler: The Full Story with New Evidence from Secret Russian Archives*.[15] Petrova and Watson were the first journalists to be shown the entire "Operation Myth" archive, including the six buff-colored files of documents, plus the charts and photographs mounted on blue boards. Finally, Petrova and Watson published photographs of Hitler's skull fragments, which had been kept unseen for decades under lock and key in a building Petrova and Watson described as "a grey, eight-story building on Bolshaya Pirogoskaya Street that some say resembles a granary tower."[16]

Petrova and Watson discovered in the archive records that the two corpses discovered in the garden of the Reich Chancellery had been moved, buried, and reburied multiple times following the autopsy conducted by the Russians in the pathology laboratory at Buch on May 8, 1945. On June 3, 1945, the secret archives documented that the bodies of Hitler, Eva Braun, the Goebbels family, and General Krebs were moved to the German province of

---

[15]   Ada Petrova and Peter Watson, *The Death of Hitler: The Full Story with New Evidence from Secret Russian Archives* (New York: W. W. Norton & Company, 1995).

[16]   Ibid., p. 76.

Brandenburg, in the vicinity of Ratenow, where they were buried at a depth of 1.7 meters (approximately 5.8 feet) in a forest near the village of Neu Friedrichsdorf. Then, on February 23, 1946, the documents indicated that the pit in the forest was dug up, and the now half-rotted corpses in their wooden box caskets were moved to the German city of Magdeburg on the Elbe River, where officials from SMERSH counter-intelligence reburied the bodies near the place of deployment of the Soviet Third Army of Occupation troops. The grave, in a courtyard at 36 Westerndstrasse, was located near the southern wall of a courtyard at a depth of 2 meters. The graves were paved over when the street was re-engineered and renamed Klausenerstrausse. There the bodies remained until 1970, when the SMERSH counter-intelligence unit was recalled to East Germany.[17]

The "Operation Myth" secret files reported that before relocating back to Russia, the head of the Soviet Third Army of Occupation stationed at Magdeburg, wanting instructions regarding the disposition of the bodies, wrote to Yuri Andropov, the future secretary general of the Russian Communist Party who was then the head of the KGB, a Soviet intelligence agency that had emerged out of preceding Soviet military intelligence units that were SMERSH competitors. On March 26, 1970, Andropov replied with orders to disinter the bodies, burn them, and dispose of the ashes. His instructions were carried out on April 4, 1970. The report on the opening of the grave read as follows: "Five wooden boxes positioned crosswise had rotted away, turned into a 'jellied mass,' the remains all mixed with earth."[18] The bone fragments of Hitler and Eva Braun had

---

[17]   Ibid., pp. 87-88.

[18]   Ibid., p. 89.

gotten mixed up with those of Krebs, the Goebbels family, and the two dogs, such that sorting them apart had become impossible. Shipped to Moscow were the four fragments of Hitler's skull and the two fragments of his jaw that Petrova and Watson found in the special archives in Moscow. On April 5, 1970, in a dump near Schönebeck, some seven miles from Magdeburg, what was left of the bodily remains were burned into embers, with the ashes scattered into one of the tributaries of the Elbe River.

Petrova and Watson also discovered that the grave in the garden of the Reich Chancellery where the bodies of Hitler and Eva Braun were originally found was in reality a pit created by an aircraft bomb, such that the fragments of the Hitler skull were found at a depth of fifty to sixty meters (some 164 to 195 feet) below ground, whereas the two bodies were found at a depth of one to two meters. The skull fragments that could easily have come from a different body altogether were associated with the Hitler corpse only because a piece of the skull was found to be missing from his body. A document in the secret file dated May 31, 1946, recorded the investigation of the skull fragments as follows:

> "Earth is attached to the fragments. The back of the skull and the temple part show signs of fire; they are charred. These fragments belong to an adult. There is an outgoing bullet hole. The shot was fired either in the mouth or the right temple at point blank range. The carbonization is the result of the fire effect, which badly damaged the corpse."[19]

The skull fragments were assumed to be Hitler's, despite the obvious bullet-hole exit wound that indicated that the person to whom the skull belonged had most likely

---

[19] Ibid., p. 85.

died from a gunshot wound. As noted above, the forensic pathologists at Buch ignored the gunshot wound evidence when they concluded that Hitler had died from cyanide poisoning.

Upon examining the autopsy records as well as the documents in the "Operation Myth" file, Petrova and Watson found that the dental evidence was not as immediately convincing as the case presented by Bezymenski. The special archive files failed to contain the detailed X-rays and dental reports Bezymenski claimed had been found. Moreover, Dr. Hugo Blaschke, Eva Braun's dentist, told the Allies that he last treated Braun in March 1945 and that her teeth were in good shape, with few fillings and no cavities. In particular, Blaschke's records indicated that the upper right molar, which was intact on the corpse, should have had a filling if it had been Braun's. Petrova and Watson concluded from the testimony of Käthe Heusermann, Dr. Blaschke's dental assistant, and Fritz Echtmann, the dental technician who claimed to have crafted a special bridge for Braun, that two identical bridges had been made, with the second held in reserve should anything go wrong with the first. Petrova and Watson were suspicious that the bridge found in Eva's mouth may have been recovered from the Chancellery dental office and placed into the mouth of the "decoy" corpse to make the Russian doctors conducting the autopsy believe the body was Braun's. That any X-rays, dental records, or back-up dentures were found in the Reich Chancellery dental office given the bomb damage from air and artillery, plus the vandalism the building suffered from Russian troops, strains credibility.

Yet in the final analysis, Petrova and Watson chose to side with the testimony of Käthe Heusermann, concluding that the recollections of Dr. Blaschke were not reliable.[20] In

---

20   Ibid., pp. 94-95.

the final analysis, they concluded that the evidence in the Moscow special archive convinced them that the bodies found were Hitler and Eva Braun.

Questions and documents

A BBC/Discovery Channel documentary, *Hitler's Death: The Final Report,* produced in 1995, raised additional questions suggesting "Operation Myth" was not the closed case that both Lev Bezymenski had argued in his 1968 blockbuster and Petrova and Watson concluded in their book published in 1995. The documentary featured British historian Norman C. Stone, former adviser to Prime Minister Margaret Thatcher, then a professor at Oxford. Moscow also gave Stone permission to study the files of "Operation Myth," including the autopsy. "In the first place, the autopsy was a bit sloppy," Stone explained on camera. "They're in a hurry. It's VE-night. The second thing is, I suspect, the fact that they [the autopsy physicians] were being leaned on by somebody simply to say, 'He [Hitler] didn't shoot himself, he munched on poison,' and that he killed his wife first of all. It sounds like good propaganda, and I suspect they [the autopsy physicians] were leaned on. Doctors in the Stalin system were leaned on. We can demonstrate it."[21] The BBC/Discovery Channel documentary further argues that Käthe Heusermann sketched a diagram of Hitler's teeth from memory, discounting that X-rays or extensive records of Hitler's dental work had been found. That Heusermann's diagram resembled almost exactly the dental specimens found during the autopsy suggested that

---

[21] The BBC and the Discovery Channel, *Hitler's Death: The Final Report – Operation Myth,* Café Productions, 1995. The BBC TV is listed as the commissioning company and The Discovery Channel is listed as the production company. Hugh Purcell, Executive Producer; Laurence Rees, Executive Producer, BBC; Dai Richards, Producer. Ian Holms, narrator.

Heusermann had been shown the dental specimens before she was asked to recreate a drawing of how she "remembered" Hitler's dental work had been done.

Stalin, refusing to accept the medical findings in Dr. Shkravaski's forensic report from the autopsy of the Hitler and Braun corpses, became enraged when Field Marshall Zhukov, the Russian hero of the Battle for Berlin, continued to make public statements that the Russians had proof Hitler and Eva Braun were dead. Stalin dispatched Andrei Vyshinsky, the notorious prosecutor from the Moscow show trials of the 1930s, to Berlin with a mission to bring Zhukov in line with his official conclusion. On June 6, 1945, with Vyshinsky at his side, Zhukov held a press conference in Berlin at which he announced, "Hitler's present whereabouts are unknown." He denied reports circulating in Berlin that the Soviets had found a corpse they were able to identify as Hitler's. "Based on personal and official information, we can only say that Hitler had a chance to get away with his bride," Zhukov told the press, adding that he now believed Hitler had fled Berlin at the very last minute. Zhukov made it clear that it was his personal view that Hitler had taken refuge in Spain.[22]

One additional point worth clarifying is evidence that Hitler used a double. In 1992, a Soviet archive film played on Russian television showing the 1945 film footage taken by Russian troops on May 4, 1945, with a corpse they assumed was Hitler with a bullet hole in the forehead. This prompted Lev Bezymenski to give an interview to the *New York Times* to set the record straight. Bezymenski told the newspaper that Andrei Smirnov, a former Soviet press attaché at Russia's embassy in Berlin who had known Hitler before the war, went to Berlin and declared that the

---

[22] Benjamin Fischer, CIA History Staff, "Hitler, Stalin, and 'Operation Myth,'" published in aboutfacts.net, 2003, http://aboutfacts.net/Else23. htm.

body that had been filmed was not Hitler's. Bezymenski explained that the film had been sent to Moscow and was erroneously included in a documentary made just after the war. "I'm absolutely sure the body in the film is not Hitler's," Bezymenski told the newspaper. "The actual body of Hitler was found in a different place, in the garden of the Chancellery, and that body was identified by a special Soviet commission as Hitler's."[23]

In 2000, the year in which Russia celebrated the 55th anniversary of the fall of Berlin, a four-inch fragment of Hitler's skull, showing the bullet hole, was for the first time put on public display, under glass at the State Archive of the Russian Federation in Moscow as part of an exhibition entitled "The Death Throes of the Third Reich: The Retribution." Also on display were trophies including Hitler's and Goebbel's personal papers, the diary of Hitler's daily activities maintained by Hitler's secretary Martin Bormann, the surrender agreement ending the Soviet-German war, several of Hitler's uniforms, and a blood-stained section of the sofa where Hitler supposedly shot himself after swallowing the cyanide capsule. No mention in the exhibit was made of the inconsistency that the autopsy conducted in Buch, Germany, on May 8, 1945, listed the cause of Hitler's death as cyanide poisoning, and made no mention of Hitler having shot himself. All these artifacts were from the State "Special Archives," as well as the holdings of the Foreign Ministry and the Russian Federal Security service.[24]

---

[23] Steven Erlanger, "Historian Asserts Soviet Soldiers Found Hitler's Charred Remains," *New York Times*, Sept. 18, 1992, http://www. nytimes.com/1992/09/18/world/historian-asserts-soviet-soldiers-found-hitler-s-charred-remains.html.

[24] Fischer, loc.cit.

That same year, in 2000, Russia permitted for the first time the publication in Moscow of an extensive collection of Hitler records, including Soviet army field reports documenting the discovery of the Hitler and Eva Braun corpses, various autopsy reports, and extensive signed statements from various eyewitnesses to Hitler's last days drawn from the "Operation Myth" files. In 2005, three Russian academics – V. K. Vinogradov, J. F. Pogonyi, and N.V. Teptozov – were given unrivalled access to the KGB Archives, including the top "Operation Myth" documents, with the goal of publishing an English translation of the Hitler files in the 2005 book entitled *Hitler's Death: Russia's Last Great Secret from the Files of the KGB.*[25] "Before the discovery of DNA, it was difficult, if not impossible, to conclusively ascertain that the charred remains found under a layer of soil in the bomb crater ten feet from the garden entrance to the Führerbunker were the corpses of Adolf Hitler and Eva Braun," British historian Andrew Roberts wrote in the foreword to the book, seemingly with prescience at what was yet to develop. "Yet the work of the Soviet intelligence services (principally SMERSH) in piecing together all the evidence for the couple's final moments—as well as the incontrovertible dental evidence set out in pages 95 to 107—put the established historical record beyond any reasonable doubts."[26]

In 2009, the conclusion that the historical record and medical forensic evidence established with scientific certainty that Hitler and Eva Braun died in Berlin as the Russian army was approaching the Reich Chancellery was forcibly challenged.

---

[25] V. K. Vinogradov, J. F. Pogonyi, and N.V. Teptozov, *Hitler's Death: Russia's Last Great Secret from the Files of the KGB* (London: Chaucer Press, 2005).

[26] Andrew Roberts, Foreword, in Vinogradov, Pogonyi, and Teptozov, op.cit., pp. 10-13, at p. 11.

The skull of a 40 year-old woman

In 2009, Mystery Quest produced a DVD-documentary for the History Channel, entitled *Hitler's Escape,* and gained permission to access the Hitler secret archives.[27] Intensive negotiations with Russian officials resulted in Dr. Nicholas Bellantoni, the state archaeologist of Connecticut, being allowed one hour to view the Hitler skull fragments (sections taken from the bloodstained couch on which Hitler supposedly shot himself) as well as the files from "Operation Myth." Bellantoni flew to Moscow to undertake the investigation, and video from the MysteryQuest documentary shows him walking into the Russian Federation State Archive building to examine the evidence.

The documentary next shows Bellantoni working in a small office within the archives building, putting on white rubber gloves and using cotton swabs to take blood samples from five different sections of the sofa, making sure to place each swab in a separate envelope to avoid cross-contamination. Next, Bellantoni can be seen examining the Hitler skull fragments. On camera, Bellantoni identifies what looks like a bullet exit wound on the skull, using his hand to point out that the skull fragment came from the occipital-parietal region of the back of the head. Using a special chart to look at bone color and cracking, Bellantoni graded the skull, determining that it showed signs of having been exposed to fire, but concluding the skull had not burned for long—certainly not long enough for a cremation. With time running out, Bellantoni took several high-resolution photographs of the skull and made various sketches. Finally,

---

[27]   MysteryQuest, *Hitler's Escape,* produced by the A&E Television Networks studio and shown first on The History Channel, September 2009. Joanna Chejade-Bloom, producer; Bill Hunt and Vincent Kralyevich, executive producers. Stan Bernard, narrator.

he gathered four samples of the skull for laboratory testing. He brought the evidence back to the genetics laboratory of the University of Connecticut Center for Applied Genetics and Technology for processing and testing.

In the documentary, Bellantoni can be seen examining the photographs of the skull fragments. His attention is drawn to the sutures connecting the skull plates, which are very open, suggesting that the skull belonged to a person who was 40 years old or younger at the time of death—not representative of the more closed zigzag sutures Bellantoni would have expected to see from Hitler, who was 56 years old when he died. The other thing Bellantoni noted was that the skull fragments were relatively small, more representative of a female skull, not the fuller, more robust fragments that Bellantoni would have expected to find from an adult male. "If the police brought us this skull, we would have thought it was a woman, to be honest with you," Bellantoni says on camera, sitting at the computer in his study. These were the first hints Bellantoni had that the skull the Russians had held for decades did not belong to Hitler at all.

Remarkably, the DNA tests conducted on the skull fragments by the University of Connecticut Center for Applied Genetics and Technology confirmed Bellantoni's suspicions. Molecular biologist Dr. Linda Strausbaugh, the director of the university center, supervised the DNA testing. Using full forensic procedures to avoid contamination, Strausbaugh and her science team, after grinding the bone fragments to powder, were able to draw DNA from the skull samples. The scientific conclusion was that the skull fragments belonged to a woman under 40 years of age whose identity was unknown. These were groundbreaking findings, calling into question the historical account of Hitler's death. "We are going to change everybody's perception, not only of these remains, but also of what happened to Adolf Hitler and others in that bunker," Bellantoni said at the conclusion of the documentary. "If this is not Adolf Hitler, who is it? And, as a result of that, we've got a lot more homework to do."

Bellantoni's scientific results were "extraordinary," the *Guardian* concluded.[28] "According to witnesses, the bodies of Hitler and Braun had been wrapped in blankets and carried to the garden just outside the Berlin bunker, placed in a bomb crater, doused with petrol, and set ablaze," writes *Guardian* reporter Uki Goñi, the author of *The Real Odessa*, a book about the escape of Nazi war criminals from Europe to Argentina.[29] "But the skull fragment the Russians dug up outside the Führerbunker in 1946 could never have belonged to Hitler. The skull DNA was incontestably female. The only positive proof that Hitler had shot himself had suddenly been rendered worthless."

The skull fragment cannot be that of Eva Braun—even though Braun was 33 years old in April 1945—simply because there is no evidence that she shot herself, and the Russian autopsy claiming to have found Braun's body concluded that she died of cyanide poising, making no mention that any part of the skull was missing. While the Russians have been much more circumspect about showing Hitler's teeth fragments, why would we believe the teeth could be dated differently, given that the Russians have always insisted the skull and teeth fragments came from the same corpse? Another problem was that the

---

[28] Uki Goñi, "Tests on skull fragment cast doubt on Adolf Hitler suicide story," *The Guardian*, Sept. 26, 2009, http://www.guardian.co.uk/world/2009/sep/27/adolf-hitler-suicide-skull-fragment.

[29] Uki Goñi, *The Real Odessa: Smuggling the Nazis to Peron's Argentina* (London: Granta Books, 2002).

DNA analysis of the blood samples taken from the sofa showed the blood was male, while the skull belonged to a woman. Lacking DNA samples from Hitler or his relatives, Bellantoni and Strausbaugh were unable to determine if the blood from the sofa belonged to him or not. But what was clear was that the blood sample from the sofa could not be tied to the exit wound observed in the female skull the Russians had for decades misidentified as Hitler's.

The Russians understandably pushed back, dismissing the DNA reports that the skull claimed by the Russians to be Hitler's was fraudulent. Vassili Khristoforov, the head of Russia's Federal Security Service, or FSB, insisted to the *Mail Online* that Russia still held authentic Hitler remains. "The FSB archives hold the jaw of Hitler and the state archives a fragment of Hitler's skull," Khristoforov told the newspaper. "With the exception of these remains, seized on May 5, 1945, there exist no other bits from the body of Hitler."[30] Yet, aside from Russian officials insisting there was no way Russia could have been deceived for nearly six decades, Russian scientists offered no counter-DNA evidence proving the skull fragments in the Moscow archives belonged to a man who was at or near Hitler's age when he died.

The point remains: scientific proof that the Russians resorted for decades to fraudulent physical "evidence" that Hitler and Eva Braun died in Berlin at the end of World War II makes virtually certain no such proof ever existed. Clearly, the Russians provided the world with the best evidence of Hitler and Eva Braun's death they could find. We return to the argument with which we began: Surely

[30] Alan Hall, "We really do have Hitler's skull, say Russians ... despite US claim bones are female," *Mail Online*, Dec. 8, 2009, http://www.dailymail.co.uk/news/article-1234131/Hitler-skull-fragments-genuine-insist-Russians.html.

if Hitler and Eva Braun had committed suicide, someone would have taken a photograph. The proof that Hitler and Eva Braun must have escaped Germany is that Russia took the best shot at proving both died without escaping the Führerbunker, only to have the suicide scenario demonstrated to be nothing more than a fabrication because the evidence upon which it was based turn out to be fraudulent. With the corpses the Russians claimed belonged to Hitler and Eva Braun conveniently cremated, with the ashes sprinkled on the Elbe River, it is now time for the Russians to show what they maintain are Hitler's dental remains.

But having had the Hitler skull proved by DNA analysis to belong to a relatively young female body, the Russians will almost certainly refuse to make the supposed Hitler dental remains public to be subjected to independent scientific examination. Why exactly the Russians have been willing to show the skull fragments while keeping the dental remains under wraps remains unknown. But when and if the Russians do decide to release the dental remains for analysis, the X-rays and dental records should be released at the same time. Independent scientific examination may be able to determine if these records are originals, or if the only dental records the Russians have come from the testimony of dental technicians recalling Hitler's dental records from memory. If there were no dental X-rays and records made by Hitler's dentist at the time the dental work was done, how could Russian officials dismiss the possibility that the dental technicians had their memories improved by first being shown the dental samples the Russians wanted identified as Hitler's?

2 | THE HITLER SUICIDE COVER STORY

The Nazi regime gave evidence of how quite literally the entire existence of the state can be based on deception. Even Hitler's death is surrounded by a fabric of lies.

—Lev Bezymenski, *The Death of Adolf Hitler* (1968)[31]

At 9:40 p.m. on Wednesday, May 2, 1945, in Germany, radio channels across the nation interrupted the dramatic playing of Wagner's "Twilight of the Gods," by the announcement, "Achtung! Achtung! The German broadcasting is going to give an important German government announcement for the German people." At 9:57 p.m. the dramatic playing of music from Wagner's "Rhinegold," with the announcer issuing another "Achtung!"

---

[31] Lev Bezymenski, *The Death of Adolf Hitler: Unknown Documents from the Soviet Archives,* op.cit., pp. 68-69.

warning calling for attention, explaining, "We are now going to play the slow movement of Bruckner's Seventh Symphony," a score written to commemorate Wagner's death.

At 10:30 p.m. in Germany—4:30 p.m. in the afternoon in New York—the music broadcast over the radio stopped. Three drum rolls preceded a moment of silence. The announcer solemnly informed the German people listening, "It is reported from Der Führer's headquarters that our Führer Adolf Hitler, fighting to the last breath against Bolshevism, fell for Germany this afternoon in his operational headquarters in the Reich Chancellery." The next speaker, identifying himself as Grand-Admiral Karl Dönitz, well known as the commander of Germany's U-boat submarine fleet, came on the radio to explain that he had been appointed as Hitler's successor. Dönitz advanced the theme that Hitler had died as a hero: "He saw the terrible dangers of Bolshevism early on and he devoted his life to the struggle against it. This struggle and his unshakably straight path was ended by his heroic death in the capital of the Reich."[32]

With this announcement, the politics of Hitler's death kicked into high gear. Immediately, the Allies began worrying that if the German people perceived Hitler as a hero fighting against communism to the death, a martyr would be born, keeping open the possibility that Nazism might once again arise in Germany. On the morning of May 3, 1945, the official Moscow radio called the German broadcast "a new Fascist trick," by which "the German Fascists evidently hope to prepare for the possibility of Hitler disappearing

---

[32] "The Appeal by Grand-Admiral Dönitz," May 2, 1945, reprinted in V. K. Vinogradov, J. F. Pogonyi, and N. V. Teptozov, *Hitler's Death*, op.cit., pp. 146-147, at p. 147.

from the scene and going to an underground position."[33] Rather than allowing Dönitz to position Hitler as having charged the ramparts in a last-ditch attempt to defend the German people, the Soviets in Moscow wanted to reframe Hitler as the culprit who abandoned Germany after leading the country into a catastrophic world war that resulted in nothing for the German people but death, destruction, and despair. The Russians appreciated that if the German people believed Hitler had escaped Berlin, their conclusion would be that Hitler was a coward who preferred to escape into hiding while Berliners had no choice but to remain in place and face captivity under the advancing Russian army.

First accounts of Hitler's death

As noted in the previous chapter, the Soviet army was the first to capture Berlin and seize the Reich Chancellery. Rushing into the Führerbunker, the first question of the Russian soldiers was, "Where is Hitler?" Failing to find him in the bunker, the Germans there explained Hitler had committed suicide and his body had been cremated outside the bunker, along with that of his wife, Eva Braun. The last chapter detailed how the Russians ultimately recovered two corpses that the Russian government ultimately tried to convince the world were the bodies of the Führer and his new wife. Stalin, as we also saw, steadfastly maintained to his death that Hitler had escaped, first to Spain and then to Argentina.

---

[33] Associated Press Report, "Nazi Report Says Hitler is Dead; Admiral Doenitz Is Announced as Successor," *Daytona Morning Journal*, Wednesday, May 2, 1945, front page, http://news.google.com/newspapers?nid=1873&dat=19450502&id=1fonAAAAIBAJ&sjid=6sYEAAAAIBAJ&pg=2038,6693743. The AP report was printed by newspapers across the United States; Dönitz's name was printed in the alternative English-language transcription as "Doenitz."

Very quietly, US military intelligence launched a full-scale investigation into Hitler's last days upon entering Berlin in late May 1945. On July 2, 1945, *Newsweek* reported that the British and the Americans were convinced Hitler was dead. "As proof, Allied headquarters released the stories of two eyewitnesses of the last days: Eric H. Kempka, Hitler's chauffeur, and Herman Karnau, one of his police sentries. The details they filled in made the Führer's death even more fantastic and gruesome than the earlier accounts." Here's how *Newsweek* described Hitler's final moments:

> Kempka, who had been Hitler's chauffeur since 1936, saw him alive for the last time on April 29, when he went to the Führer's bunker and reported how he had brought food and supplies to the various command posts. Hitler, he said, seemed "quiet and normal."
>
> At 2:40 on April 30, continued Kempka, Guensche [one of Hitler's bodyguards] went into Hitler's room. There in front of him, grotesquely sprawled together over the couch, were the bodies of the Führer and his wife [Eva Braun], dead in a suicide pact. On the floor in front of Hitler lay a 7.65-millimeter Walther pistol; he had been shot through the head. Eva had a bullet through her heart, and near the couch was a smaller-caliber Walther.[34]

The *Newsweek* article continued, detailing how Martin Bormann, Hitler's secretary, had helped Kempka and Heinz Linge, Hitler's personal valet, carry the bodies of Hitler and Eva Braun outside the bunker into the Reich Chancellery garden. There, the bodies were placed into "a shallow hole"

---

[34] "Hitler: The Cremation," *Newsweek*, July 2, 1945, p. 24. Parentheses were added to the original for clarification.

and unidentified "men" arrived with five cans of gasoline that were poured on the bodies. "Bormann, Goebbels [Reich Minister of Propaganda], Linge, I, and a couple of others stood at attention and gave the Hitler salute," Kempka told *Newsweek*, explaining that there was no elaborate ceremony because Russian artillery shells were coming in from all sides. "Guensche, carrying out Hitler's last order, set the bodies afire. We stayed a couple of minutes and went back to the shelter. We left a single guard to watch the fire. He was a security policeman whom I did not know. I doubt if anything remained of the bodies. The fire was terrifically intense." *Newsweek* gave the date of the cremation as May 1. Kempka added that he doubted any evidence of Hitler or Eva Braun's bodies would ever be found, except for some bits of bone and teeth. "Shells probably landed there and scattered everything all over."

By October 1945, the US investigation was derailed, with the announcement that the British were sending a young historian to Berlin to write a book.

Enter Trevor-Roper

On Oct. 1, 1945, the US Army issued a typewritten notice documenting that the British army had called to say a Major Trevor-Roper from British military intelligence in London was in Berlin at the request of British Brigadier Dick White, then head of counter-intelligence in the British sector of Berlin, to conduct an inquiry regarding Hitler's death.[35] The following day, the Headquarters of the US Forces, European Theater, Office of the Assistant Chief of

---

[35] US Army, typewritten instructions, no title, dated Oct. 1, 1945. National Archives and Records Administration (NARA), Silver Spring, MD, Reg. No. 319, Stack Area 270, Row 84, Compartment 7, Entry (A1) 134-B, Personal Name File, Boxes 295-297.

Staff, G-2, issued a bearer-memorandum for Major Trevor-Roper to carry with him in the field, asking US military personnel approached by Trevor-Roper to assist him "to the fullest possible extent, including providing facilities for interrogating those persons, as named by him, who may have information relating to subject inquiry."[36]

As noted earlier, Trevor-Roper in 1945 was a history graduate student at Oxford who had been recruited to work in military intelligence during the war. In his career after the war, as Regius Professor of Modern History at Oxford, Trevor-Roper was faulted for not writing a major work of history and leaving behind a "biography studded with abandoned manuscripts and unfulfilled publisher's contracts."[37] In 1983, he fell into disgrace when the German magazine *Stern* asked him to authenticate the so-called Hitler Diaries. Trevor-Roper staked his reputation on his judgment that the diaries were authentic. He suffered international embarrassment when the diaries were proven to be a forgery, but only after *The Sunday Times*, a publication to which Trevor-Roper was a regular contributor and an independent director, paid a considerable sum to obtain the rights to serialize the diaries.[38] This scandal so sullied Trevor-Roper's career that when *The Times* in

---

[36] Headquarters of the US Forces, European Theater, Office of the Assistant Chief of Staff, G-2, "Subject: Investigation of Circumstances Surrounding the Death of Adolf Hitler," Oct. 2, 1945, signed Dupre Sassard, Lt. Col., GSC Executive. NARA, op.cit., see footnote #4.

[37] Stefan Collini, "Hugh Trevor-Roper: The Biography by Adam Sisman," *The Guardian*, July 16, 2010, http://www.guardian.co.uk/books/2010/jul/17/hugh-trevor-roper-biography-review.

[38] Robert Harris, *Selling Hitler: The Extraordinary Story of the Con Job of the Century – The Faking of the Hitler "Diaries"* (New York: Pantheon, 1986).

London published his obituary, the headline was: "Hitler diary hoax victim [Trevor-Roper] dies at 89," making no mention of his wartime work investigating Hitler's death for British intelligence.[39]

In 1947, Trevor-Roper published the results of his investigation in *The Last Days of Hitler*,[40] a short book that received international acclaim and established for decades the "authoritative" account of Hitler's death.

Trevor-Roper's account of Hitler's demise

Trevor-Roper begins by relating an account of how Hitler reacted to Mussolini's death.

> Captured by partisans during the general uprising of northern Italy, Mussolini and his mistress Clara Petacci had been executed, and their bodies suspended by the feet in the marketplace of Milan to be beaten and pelted by the vindictive crowd. If the full details were ever known to them, Hitler and Eva Braun could only have repeated the orders they had already been given; their bodies were to be destroyed "so that nothing remains"; "I will not fall into the hands of an enemy who requires a new spectacle to divert his hysterical masses."[41]

With this passage, Trevor-Roper introduced the idea that Hitler preferred to kill himself rather than end up

---

[39]   Stefan Collini, *Hugh Trevor-Roper: The Biography by Adam Sisman*, loc.cit.

[40]   H. R. Trevor-Roper, *The Last Days of Hitler* (New York: The Macmillan Company, 1947).

[41]   Ibid., p. 196.

becoming a spectacle like Mussolini had become after his death. But notice how cleverly he has written this passage. Truthfully, he had no evidence that Hitler knew anything about how Mussolini and Clara Petacci died. The key phrase in the passage above is this: "If the full details were ever known to them …" What this signaled is that Trevor-Roper knew upon entering into the discussion of Hitler's death that he was speculating, providing a fictional account. Obviously, Trevor-Roper did this only because he did not have the evidence to prove what Hitler was thinking in what Trevor-Roper wanted the reader to conclude were his final hours.

In the next few pages, Trevor-Roper described how Hitler had Professor Haase, his surgeon, put down his favorite Alsatian dog, Blondi. Hitler had the occupants of the bunker line up so he could shake hands with them and bid a final solemn goodbye. "He [Hitler] walked in silence down the passage and shook hands with all the women in turn," Trevor-Roper wrote, describing the Führer as appearing drugged.[42] Trevor-Roper wrote that all the participants in this strange drama knew it could only mean one thing: "The terrible sorcerer, the tyrant who had charged their days with intolerable melodrama tension, would soon be gone, and for a brief twilight they could play."[43] The play involved the occupants of the bunker breaking out into a brief dancing episode. Again, notice how Trevor-Roper used this detail to build the tension by demonstrating how those sharing the bunker with Hitler knew the end was near for the tyrant. Trevor-Roper's writing building up to Hitler's

---

[42] Ibid., p. 197. Parenthesis added for clarity.

[43] Ibid., p. 198.

dual suicide with Eva Braun was emotion-laden, subtly drawing the reader into the presumption that Hitler had to have committed suicide, otherwise the events he was describing made no sense.

Trevor-Roper's narrative picked up the next morning, April 30, 1945, with Hitler's bodyguard and adjutant Sturmbannfuehrer Otto Guensche ordering Hitler's chauffeur Strumbannfuehrer Erich Kempka to go fetch 200 gallons of petrol, lying that the fuel was needed for a ventilating plant that was oil-driven. Obviously, the petrol would not have been needed if there weren't bodies to cremate. Next, Trevor-Roper has Hitler and Eva Braun hold a "farewell ceremony" with the top officials yet remaining in the bunker, including Hitler's secretary Martin Bormann and his Minister of Propaganda Joseph Goebbels. Following this, Hitler and Eva Braun return to their private suite. Then comes the climactic passage:

> The others were dismissed, all but the high priests and those few others whose services would be necessary. They waited in the passage. A single shot was heard. After an interval they entered the suite. Hitler was lying on the sofa, which was soaked with blood. He had shot himself through the mouth. Eva Braun was also on the sofa, also dead. A revolver was by her side, but she had not used it; she had swallowed poison. The time was half-past three.[44]

Again, the account of Hitler's suicide is skillfully written to hide what Trevor-Roper truthfully does not know. Notice, Trevor-Roper omitted stating exactly who went into the suite to discover the dead bodies, and who waited outside. Next, Trevor-Roper described that Arthur

---

[44] Ibid., p. 201.

Axmann, the head of the Hitler Youth, arrived in the bunker and was allowed to view the bodies. Trevor-Roper has Axmann and Goebbels exchange a few words before Goebbels departs, leaving Axmann alone in the suite with the bodies.

Outside the bunker, we are told Hitler's minions were preparing what Trevor-Roper described as "another ceremony," namely, "the Viking funeral."[45] Inside the bunker, Guensche told Kempka, "The Chief is dead," while Hitler's adjutant, Heinz Linge, wrapped Hitler's body in a blanket to conceal "the bloodstained and shattered head." Trevor-Roper was careful to add a detail that "other observers" supposedly recognized that the body had to be Hitler's because they easily recognized Hitler's familiar black trousers.

Trevor-Roper next had two S.S. officers carry Hitler's body up the four flights of stairs to the emergency exit and out into the garden. After this, Trevor-Roper had Bormann enter Hitler's private room to take up Eva Braun's body. "Her death had been tidier, and no blanket was needed to conceal the evidence of it," Trevor-Roper wrote, making it clear that those in the bunker who saw the female body before it was cremated recognized the body as Eva Braun's. Trevor-Roper noted that Bormann took Eva Braun's body to the foot of the stairs, where it was handed to Guensche, with Guensche handing the body in turn to a third unidentified S.S. officer who carried Eva Braun's body upstairs to the garden.[46]

So, now that the two main characters have been eliminated by suicide, with Trevor-Roper taking pains to identify

---

[45]   Ibid.

[46]   Ibid., p. 202.

witnesses who could identify the bodies, all that remained for him to do was to describe how identifiable witnesses knew the bodies that were cremated beyond recognition were Hitler and Eva Braun. To accomplish this, Trevor-Roper conveniently added to the narrative two uninvited witnesses outside who both supposedly recognized Hitler and Eva Braun before the bodies were cremated.

Outside the bunker, police guard Erich Mansfield, on duty in the concrete observation tower at the corner of the bunker, decided to investigate. Before scurrying back to his tower, Mansfield watched the funeral procession emerge from the bunker, according to Trevor-Roper's account. "First there were two S.S. officers carrying a body wrapped in a blanket, with black-trousered legs protruding from it," Trevor-Roper wrote, describing the scene now supposedly through Mansfield's eyes. "Then there was another S.S. officer carrying the unmistakable corpse of Eva Braun."[47] Trailing out of the bunker last were the mourners, including Bormann, Goebbels, Guensche, Linge, Kempka, and Wehrmacht general Wilhelm Burgdorf, one of the last remaining military generals loyal to Hitler. Trevor-Roper wrote that the corpses became enveloped in a sheet of flame, while the mourners came to attention and gave the Hitler salute before they slipped back in to the safety of the bunker to escape the Russian bombardment.

Next, the two corpses were supposedly placed side-by-side and petrol was poured over them. Guensche dipped a rag in petrol, set it alight, and threw it out on the corpses. Police guard Hermann Karnau, the second uninvited spectator, came accidentally on to the scene as the cremation

---

[47]   Ibid.

was in progress. "Karnau watched the burning corpses for a moment," Trevor-Roper related. "They were easily recognizable, though Hitler's head was smashed. The sight, he says, was 'repulsive in the extreme.'" The corpses, according to Trevor-Roper's account, burned for hours until a Russian artillery shell scored a direct hit, creating a crater that conveniently became the grave for whatever remained of the bodies.

Trevor-Roper concluded the narrative with the following observation:

> That is all that is known about the disposal of the remnants of Hitler's and Eva Braun's bodies. Linge afterwards told one of the secretaries that they had been burned, as Hitler had ordered, "'till nothing remained"; but it is doubtful whether such total combustion would have taken place. One hundred and eighty litres of petrol, burning slowly on a sandy bed, would char the flesh and dissipate the moisture of the bodies, leaving only an unrecognizable and fragile remainder; but the bones would withstand the heat. These bones have never been found.[48]

Trevor-Roper commented that the Russians "have occasionally dug in that garden," but many bodies were found there and Trevor-Roper expressed doubt the Russians could possibly have recovered Hitler and Eva Braun's corpses.[49] Trevor-Roper concludes the account lyrically: "Whatever the explanation, Hitler achieved his last ambition. Like Alaric, buried secretly under the river-bed of Busento, the modern destroyer of mankind is now

---

[48] Ibid., p. 205.

[49] Ibid., p. 206.

immune from discovery."[50] With that, Trevor-Roper completes the narrative, concluding that Hitler accomplished his goal in that the Russians never discovered his body to expose the corpse to derision and ridicule. Trevor-Roper wrote the account conveniently so that we are convinced because of the witnesses that Hitler was not only dead, but also gone, and there was no way the Russians could have recovered his body.

What the careful reader would note is that by admitting Hitler's body was not discovered, Trevor-Roper has just admitted there is no physical proof that Hitler died. For all we know, Trevor-Roper's entire account could have been fictional. This is what Trevor-Roper's detractors have argued since his book was first published in 1947.

What Trevor-Roper neglects to tell the reader is that the Russians prohibited him from interviewing the witnesses in the bunker that they had taken prisoner. Yet, Trevor-Roper describes the actions of Linge and Kempka as if he was certain what he wrote about their actions was in fact what they did. The Americans, who had orders to cooperate with the British investigation, allowed Trevor-Roper access to the written accounts of American military interviews with the bunker witnesses held prisoner by the Americans.[51] BBC journalist Robert Harris, while investigating Trevor-Roper's role regarding the Hitler Diaries, concluded that he only managed to interview in person seven witnesses who were with Hitler during the final months of his life, including the chauffeur, Erich Kempka, who obtained the gasoline for Hitler's

---

[50] Ibid.

[51] Simon Dunstan and Gerrard Williams, *Grey Wolf: The Escape of Adolf Hitler – The Case Presented* (New York: Sterling, 2011), pp. xxi – xxii.

cremation ceremony, and the guard Hermann Karnau who ended up witnessing the bodies of Hitler and Eva Braun being placed in the pit in the Chancellery garden and the cremation ceremony that followed.[52]

Bormann was nowhere to be found, and Goebbels as well as his wife and children were dead in what amounted to a family suicide. Clearly, if Trevor-Roper had conducted more interviews himself, he could have begun his book with a dramatic and detailed account of Hitler's death in which he quoted eyewitness testimony word-for-word. This he did not do. Instead, in a book of 254 pages dedicated to the final days of the Führer, Trevor-Roper devoted only 10 pages at the end of the book to delivering an emotionally written story of how Hitler and Eva Braun had committed suicide together that he must have assumed would be believable, as long as Hitler stayed missing.

Also little questioned when his book was published in 1947 was why Trevor-Roper had changed the account of the suicides from what *Newsweek* published in the month following Hitler's presumed death. In Trevor-Roper's account, Hitler shoots himself in the mouth and Eva Braun takes poison. Yet in *Newsweek's* account, Hitler shot himself "through the head" and Eva Braun shot herself through the heart.

Hitler's suicide: a judge investigates for the United States

In 1950, attorney and jurist Michael Musmanno published *Ten Days to Die*, an account of Hitler's last days

---

[52] Robert Harris, *Selling Hitler: The Extraordinary Story of the Con Job of the Century – the Faking of the Hitler "Diaries"* (New York: Pantheon Books, 1986), p. 44.

based on the dozens of interrogations of Hitler associates that he conducted while he lead the US investigation to determine whether Hitler died at the end of World War II.[53] Musmanno had served as naval aide to General Mark Clark, Fifth Army, during the US invasion of Italy. After the war, Musmanno served as presiding judge in the Nuremberg International Military Tribunal trials brought in 1947 and 1948 against officers of the *Einsatzgruppen*— SS mobile death squads that fought behind the front lines in Eastern Europe from 1941 to 1943 and were prosecuted for the mass murder of over one million Jews. Musmanno ended his career as a justice of the Pennsylvania Supreme Court. While he was also denied direct access to interrogate the Hitler associates held prisoner by the Russians, he had much more access to eyewitnesses to Hitler's last days who were not in Russian captivity. Taking three years to conduct the interviews for his 1950 book from a wide range of Nazis, including prominent Nazis such as Hitler's successor Admiral Dönitz, Hitler's secretaries, and of course Erich Kempka. In total, the Gumberg Library Digital Collection at Duquesne University has archived the original typed transcripts of over 65 interviews Musmanno conducted prior to 1950 with Nazi associates of Hitler, including as mentioned several who had participated in-person in Hitler's last days in the Führerbunker.[54]

In Musmanno's account of Hitler's death, he acknowledged that he did not know precisely why Hitler committed

---

[53] Michael A. Musmanno, *Ten Days to Die* (Garden City, N.Y.: Doubleday & Company, 1950).

[54] "Musmanno Collection – Interrogations of Hitler Associates," Gumberg Library Digital Collections, Duquesne University, http://digital.library.duq.edu/cdm-musmanno/.

suicide. "He [Hitler] does not want to die," Musmanno wrote, describing the scene in which Hitler shakes hands to say goodbye to those in the bunker just before the final moments. "If he dies for anything, he dies for fear—fear of the Russians, fear of the disclosure that he is a corporal after all—so he confines his final remarks on the platform of life to directions to the stage manager about what to do with the papier-mâché figure left on his hands after the curtain goes down."[55] Musmanno reported that Hitler had left the final arrangements about disposing of his body to Otto Guensche, his persona adjutant. Interestingly, Guensche was imprisoned by the Soviets on May 2, 1945, and remained in Russian prison and labor camps until he was released in 1956.

But to continue Musmanno's narrative, Guensche is described as accompanying Hitler and Eva Braun into what Musmanno describes as "their apartment" in the Führerbunker; Hitler nods knowingly to Guensche as he exits, closing the door behind him.[56] Standing outside Hitler's private rooms, Musmanno named the following Hitler associates as waiting: Hitler's secretary Martin Bormann, minister of propaganda Joseph Goebbels, Wehrmacht general Hans Krebs, leader of the Hitler Youth Arthur Axmann, and Wehrmacht general Wilhelm Burgdorf. Once they heard the pistol shot, Musmanno reports Axmann, followed by Goebbels, was the first to enter, as Guensche stepped aside. What they found is that Hitler committed suicide by a pistol shot through his mouth after he had bit on a cyanide capsule, and Eva Braun died from having ingested cyanide poison. Trevor-Roper

---

[55] Ibid., pp. 215-216.

[56] Ibid., p. 216.

agrees that Hitler shot himself in the head, but he neglects to note that Hitler had also bitten down on the cyanide capsule.

Here is Musmanno's word-for-word account of what Axmann and Goebbels found inside:

> Hitler, sitting on the sofa, arms dangling, has fallen forward on a little table from which his head, mouth agape, is dripping blood onto the rug, which absorbs it like a parched soil which has waited long for water. His pistol (the same Walther 7.65) lies on the floor to his right. His most recent acquisition, Eva Braun, has paid the price that so many have paid who loved him too well. Her mouth is half open, her eyes half shut, and her head inclines on his left shoulder. Her pistol (a Walther 6.35) is also at her feet, unfired. Nevertheless, there is no breath in Eva's nostrils.[57]

Musmanno detailed Hitler's fatal shot graphically: "The blast of the pistol shot's explosion in his mouth ruptured the veins on either side of his forehead."[58] Given this account, the couch on which Hitler sat and the walls of the bunker would have been splattered with Hitler's brain matter and blood.

In Musmanno's account, Hitler's valet, Heinz Linge, wraps Hitler's head and upper body in a blanket and carries him out. Bormann gathers up Eva Braun and hands her over to Kempka. The group climbs the stairs out of the bunker into the garden above. Guensche and Kempka grab the petrol cans Kempka had gathered up earlier in the day, and proceed to douse Hitler's and Eva Braun's bodies

57   Ibid., p. 219.

58   Ibid.

with gasoline. Musmanno agreed with Trevor-Roper that Russian artillery shells created a grave that covered the two char-burned corpses. "There never was any authoritative account that Hitler's and Eva Braun's bodies were ever found," Musmanno concluded, declaring as a fraud the Russian assertion to the contrary.[59] Yet somehow, the Russian army, as we saw in the last chapter, claimed to have both bodies.

Eyewitnesses tell different stories

Lev Bezymenski's 1968 book, *The Death of Adolf Hitler: Unknown Documents from the Soviet Archives*, not only raised questions about the autopsies: The book made it clear that the Führerbunker eyewitnesses who were captured by the Russians were subjected to several years of repetitive, brutal interrogation techniques involving food and sleep deprivation, as well as constant subjugation to freezing jail cells without adequate clothing or bedding to protect against the cold. As a result, the German prisoners appeared to tell their Russian interrogators whatever they perceived the Russians wanted to hear. Bezymenski made it apparent that the eyewitness testimony was essentially worthless by producing a simple chart that compared the two different stories told by Hitler's bodyguard and adjutant Otto Guensche (one in 1950 and another in 1960), a third story told by Hitler's valet Heinz Linge, a fourth story told by Erich Kempka, Hitler's chauffeur, and a fifth version as reported by author Trevor-Roper.[60]

---

[59] Ibid., p. 233.

[60] Bezymenski, *The Death of Hitler*, op.cit., p. 71.

	Guensche (1950)	**Guensche (1960)**	**Linge**
Position of the bodies of Hitler and Eva Braun	Sitting next to each other on the sofa	Hitler in chair, sitting, Braun lying in chair	Sitting at opposite sides of the sofa (Braun left)
Entry of shot in Hitler	Right temple	No particulars	Left temple

	Erich Kempka	**Trevor-Roper**
Position of the bodies of Hitler and Eva Braun	On sofa (Hitler lying, Braun sitting)	Lying next to each other on sofa
Entry of shot in Hitler	Mouth	Mouth

"The confusion and lack of uniformity in the statements indicate that the collaborators who managed to escape from the bunker purposely tried to hide the truth in order to foster the legend that the Führer had shot himself like a man," Bezymenski concluded.[61] As we noted in the first chapter, Bezymenski argued that the Germans wanted to portray Hitler's death in as heroic a manner as possible, while the Russians preferred to portray Hitler as having taken the cowardly way, biting down on a cyanide capsule because he lacked the courage to pull the trigger on himself. Bezymenski does not seriously consider another possibility, namely, that the stories varied because all the

---

[61]   Ibid., pp. 71-71.

eyewitness were fabricating the dual suicide scenario, in an effort to cover up the truth that Hitler and Eva Braun had escaped.

The shot nobody heard

In 1978, journalist James P. O'Donnell published *The Bunker: The History of the Reich Chancellery Group*, based on his firsthand experience with the Führerbunker and his interviews with fifty surviving eyewitnesses to Hitler's final hours.[62] Having served as a Signal Corps intelligence officer with the US Army in World War II, O'Donnell was discharged on July 2, 1945, at which point he accepted a job as *Newsweek*'s bureau chief.

On July 4, 1945, after arriving in Berlin, O'Donnell bribed the two Soviet soldiers guarding the Führerbunker with a gift of American cigarettes, thus becoming one of the first Americans to gain entrance to the underground chambers. Once inside, O'Donnell was surprised to find a treasure trove of Nazi documents, including Hitler's day-book, which had been overlooked by the Soviets in their mad dash to find Hitler's body.

It was not until 1972, more than a quarter-century after the end of World War II, that O'Donnell returned to Germany to conduct some fifty in-person interviews between 1972 and 1976 with those eyewitnesses to Hitler's final days who were still alive and able to speak intelligently about their experiences with Hitler. "From the beginning of my long journey down the *autobahn* into the past, I realized I was operating on the very outer fringes of time and

---

62   James P. O'Donnell, *The Bunker: The History of the Reich Chancellery Group* (Boston: Houghton Mifflin Company, 1978).

human memory, including my own," O'Donnell honestly admitted.[63]

One of the most startling revelations in O'Donnell's book comes from Erich Kempka, who admitted that he was not in the bunker to hear any shot fired, undermining the testimony that accounts since the event (including the "authoritative" account rendered by Trevor-Roper) had relied upon to be truthful. Kempka told O'Donnell that when Hitler and Eva Braun killed themselves, he was just returning from the mission to bring back the gasoline that Major Guensche had sent him to find. Here was Kempka's story in 1974, when O'Donnell interviewed him:

> Yes, Major Guensche is right. He had sent me off to round up at least two hundred liters of gasoline, ten jerry cans, but I was able to find only six or seven in my Reich Chancellery garage. I "pumped" [that is, borrowed] two more from Cheftechniker Hentschel. I was thus on my way back to the Führerbunker when I met up with the funeral cortège. That lout Bormann was carrying the body of Eva Braun, clutching her breast with his apelike paw. Somehow this maddened me. He was carrying her as if she were a sack of potatoes. Just as they all started to ascend the staircase, I reached the bottom. So, I grabbed the body of Eva Braun Hitler from Bormann and began to carry her up the stairs myself. I think if Bormann had resisted my effort, I would have hauled off and clobbered him, but he made no protest.[64]

---

63   Ibid., p. 17.

64   Ibid., p. 226. Brackets in original.

When O'Donnell asked Kempka why his story had changed, Kempka responded, "That was 1945. It is now 1974. So let me level with you. Back in '45, to save my own skin, I told American and British interrogators just about anything or everything I thought they wanted to hear. Since they kept grilling me about 'that shot' I finally told them that I heard it. It seemed to make things easier."[65] O'Donnell described Kempka, who died in 1975, as "a primitive, vulgar, thoroughly unpleasant man," who was a notorious drinker that liked to brag about his numerous sexual conquests.[66]

The 2009 documentary, *Hitler's Escape*, sent experts into the Führerbunker to determine whether the construction of the facility would have permitted a shot to be heard with the door closed to Hitler's private rooms. The conclusion was that if the thickness of the walls and the construction of the bunker prevented the loud noise of the diesel generators used in the bunker to produce electricity from being heard, then it was extremely unlikely a pistol shot within the private rooms with the door closed could have been heard by those standing in the hallway outside.[67]

Hitler doppelgängers

In 1995, British physician Hugh Thomas, an expert on gunshot wounds, published *The Murder of Adolf Hitler: The*

---

[65]   Ibid.

[66]   Ibid., p. 227.

[67]   MysteryQuest, *Hitler's Escape*, produced by the A&E Television Networks studio and shown first on The History Channel, September 2009, loc.cit.

Truth about the Bodies in the Berlin Bunker, in which he directly grappled with the evidence that the corpses found in the Führerbunker were doppelgängers—stand-in doubles for Hitler and Eva Braun—and explored whether the eyewitness testimony of Hitler's last hours was so conflicting and contradictory as to suggest the eyewitnesses were covering up a deeper crime.[68]

Thomas dismissed the corpses the Russians found, noting that in the toxicological tests there was no evidence of cyanide residue, or any other poison, in the tissues of "Hitler's body," and that cause of death in the "Eva Braun" corpse was found to be due to a massive shrapnel wound in the chest. That the dental records match in both instances, Thomas attributed to dental fixtures being forged such that duplicate dentures were manufactured for Eva Braun and shoved in the mouth of the female corpse, while for Hitler a jaw was manufactured to recreate the dental bridges documented in his dental records, as well as in the five X-ray plates of Hitler's head allegedly belonging to his physicians Dr. Theodor Morell and Erwin Giesing that were found in the US National Archives in 1972.[69]

Regarding the eyewitness testimony, Thomas was equally dismissive. "The whole story of the alleged suicides of Hitler and Eva in the Bunker is totally farcical," he wrote. "The testimony of every single witness is badly tainted; not

---

[68] Hugh Thomas, *The Murder of Adolf Hitler: The Truth about the Bodies in the Berlin Bunker* (New York: St. Martin's Press, 1995); published first in Great Britain under the title, *Doppelgängers: The Truth about the Bodies in the Berlin Bunker* (London: Fourth Estate Limited, 1995).

[69] Ibid., Chapter 3, "The Discovery of the Corpses – Forensic Fraud," pp. 123 – 151, with particular attention to p. 150.

one witness is credible. There is, moreover, a far greater than normal incidence of changed testimony. This could be partially explained by several factors: the need for conformity, media pressure, or monetary gain."[70] Noting that by 1995 there were in print "a considerable number of conflicting testimonies" about precisely how Hitler and Eva Braun died, Thomas discredited all eyewitness accounts with the following: "Some of these [eyewitness accounts] are confused, some are deliberately duplicitous; very few are unchanged."[71]

Realizing that Kempka admitted in 1974 that he had lied forced Thomas to reevaluate the claimed "authenticity" of Trevor-Roper's 1947 book, *The Last Days of Hitler.* The truth was that Kempka was not even in the bunker when Hitler and Eva Braun supposedly committed suicide, so it was impossible for Kempka to have heard a pistol shot. As a consequence, Thomas dismissed Hugh Trevor-Roper's 1947 book and the entire British propaganda campaign that accompanied the publication of the book as fiction at best, "based on the false testimony of one man."[72]

Thomas speculated that Eva Braun had tried unsuccessfully to kill herself by cutting her wrists. He imagined that Linge offered Hitler a cyanide capsule and the use of his pistol, but when Hitler refused to kill himself, Lange obliged him by strangling Hitler to death. After reviving Eva Braun, the conspirators in the bunker helped her escape, Thomas explained. What makes this hypothesis

---

[70]   Ibid., p. 112.

[71]   Ibid., p. 90. Brackets added for clarity.

[72]   Ibid., p. 96.

interesting is that Thomas thought the alternative that the eyewitnesses in the bunker had conspired to murder Hitler was the only way to explain why their testimony was so contradictory.

The puzzle Thomas was trying to solve was why all the countless hours of eyewitness testimony taken at the end of the war by American, British, and Russian intelligence, and subsequently over several decades by credible authors and journalists, amounted to nothing more than storytelling. What Thomas is trying to cope with is answering the riddle about why those close to Hitler in his final days and hours would go to such lengths to convince the world that they had witnessed Hitler's suicide. But instead of trying to cover up a murder, one equally plausible explanation that Thomas did not consider is that none of the Nazi witnesses wanted to let on about their complicity in allowing Hitler and Eva Braun to escape.

While the accounts told by the various eyewitnesses vary significantly in important details—so much so as to make none of the accounts believable—the eyewitnesses generally adhered to the same basic story. In all the accounts, Hitler and Eva Braun enter their private rooms in the Führerbunker and kill themselves in one way or another by pistol shots, cyanide capsules, or some combination. Both are discovered dead. Their bodies are taken outside and cremated. Clearly, the only solution for the eyewitnesses that would end the investigation by closing the case depended upon the world believing that Hitler had died in the Führerbunker, unable to escape Berlin.

If the eyewitnesses in the Führerbunker were guilty of a conspiracy, it is unlikely to have been a conspiracy to murder Hitler. More likely, the conspiracy was arranged for all to tell their version of the Hitler suicide story. If the eyewitnesses in the Führerbunker were found to have been co-conspirators in the effort to get Hitler and Eva Braun safely out of Berlin, who knows what reprisals the Allies, and especially the Russians, might have visited upon them? While not precisely a capital crime, helping the most genocidal maniac the world had ever known to escape would have been a crime not easily excused, especially not in the immediate aftermath of World War II and the Holocaust it occasioned.

3

"WHERE IS ADOLF HITLER?"

Why, then, is it generally accepted that Hitler is dead? No one in the west ever saw Hitler's corpse.

—Glenn B. Infield, *Hitler's Secret Life* (1979)[73]

"Where is Adolf Hitler?" was the only question asked by the first Soviet Union troops to enter the Führerbunker.

Not finding the Führer there, the victorious Russian soldiers ransacked the place. US Army Signal Corps intelligence officer James P. O'Donnell, when he arrived at the Führerbunker on July 4, 1945, two months later, was shocked to find there was nothing of any intrinsic value left. "No full liquor bottles, no usable weapons, no blankets or articles of clothing, no dress daggers, radios,

---

[73] Glenn B. Infield, *Hitler's Secret Life: The Mysteries of the Eagle's Nest* (New York: Stein and Day, 1979), p. 278.

or cameras."[74] Describing the abandoned bunker as looking like "the Paris flea market after an auction sale," O'Donnell was shocked to find a mass of printed material still in the bunker—military telephone books and telephone-number pads, loose-leaf notebooks, business office files and dossiers, Hitler's appointment book and Martin Bormann's personal diary, military manuals, scratch pads, and letters.

What was wrong with this picture? O'Donnell noted that the Germans had always been meticulous in destroying even minor pieces of evidence, and above all, printed matter, when abandoning a headquarters or signal center. "Whenever they had time, they [the Nazi military] had usually blown up a signal center," he wrote. "Bored soldiers make doodles and jottings on paper. This habit can betray a code, a radio frequency, a call sign."[75]

O'Donnell concluded the Russians had committed "an intelligence oversight of major importance."[76] But the reason was easily discerned. "At least five Red Army search teams had been in the bunker the day it fell," he noted. "They had been looking for only one thing: the body."

Photographic evidence

William Vandivert, then a 33-year-old *Life* magazine photographer, was the first Western photographer to gain access to the Führerbunker on July 3, 1945.[77] Vandivert

---

[74] James P. O'Donnell, *The Bunker: The History of the Reich Chancellery Group*, op.cit., p. 11.

[75] Ibid.

[76] Ibid., p. 12.

[77] "After the Fall: Photos of Hitler's Bunker and the Ruins of Berlin," featuring photographs taken by *Life* magazine's William Vandivert, life.time.com, no date, http://life.time.com/history/adolf-hitler-bunker-and-the-ruins-of-berlin-1945/#1.

followed *Life* magazine correspondent Percy Knauth and two other army-uniformed war correspondents with his camera as they inspected the Führerbunker and the garden area in the Reich Chancellery above.

One of the more important photos taken inside the bunker shows the three correspondents inspecting a couch stained with blood by candlelight. What is startling is that the bloodstain forms little more than a narrow streak on the left arm of the couch with what appears to be some staining of the seat cushion immediately below the left arm. But if this is where Hitler sat to shoot himself in the mouth, the physical evidence does not support the conclusion that he killed himself with any pistol shot to the head, regardless of whether he shot himself in the right temple, left temple, or mouth. Self-inflicted pistol shots to the head are typically inflicted at point-blank range, with the pistol pressed directly against the side of the head or inserted into the mouth. The resulting exit wound sends a broad spew of brain tissue, blood, and bone out the side or back of the head, typically at high velocity, creating a massive splatter pattern on whatever objects are in the path. In this particular photo, there is no splatter from the head wound visible on the couch or the corner walls against which the couch was pushed. There are no indications whatsoever of blood stains on the other arm of the couch or on the wall behind, making it extremely unlikely that Eva Braun killed herself with a pistol shot to the heart while sitting there. Except for the one streak of blood mentioned above, the couch and the room where the couch was found are devoid altogether of bloodstains on the walls or floor.

Another photograph, not originally published in the magazine, shows the correspondents in the garden area outside the bunker, crouching as they examine a shallow trench where, the correspondents had been told, the bodies of Hitler and Eva Braun were burned after their suicides. The problem with this photograph is that the ditch does not look wide enough for two bodies to be placed side-by-side, and the debris in the trench suggests no bodies had been placed there head-to-toe. Moreover, there is no indication the ground had been burned by the gasoline-fueled fire described by various eyewitnesses who had supposedly viewed the bodies of Hitler and Eva Braun being cremated there. Nor is there any evidence from the relatively ordered wood debris filling the garden around the ditch that the area was ever subjected to the type of heavy artillery bombardment needed to have destroyed and buried the bodies in a series of direct hits that dislodged enough surrounding earth to create craters and fill graves. Interestingly, in his typed notes describing these photographs, Vandivert inserted by hand the word "supposedly" into the typewritten sentence, so that it read with the addition as follows: " ... closeup of ditch where Hitler and Eva 'supposedly' burned."

A third picture that shows Knauth and the other two army correspondents entering a door leading down to the bunker gives a more panoramic view of the garden area, making it clear that the area has not experienced massive bomb or artillery damage. Except for the shallow ditch observed in the second photo, there are no bomb craters visible. The garden observed in this third photograph bears no resemblance to the artillery-bombarded garden described in the eyewitness testimony discussed in the previous chapter.

A subsequent fourth photograph, also not originally published in *Life*, shows three empty gasoline cans that the photograph caption says were reportedly used by SS troops to burn the bodies of Hitler and Eva Braun. No other gasoline cans are visible in any of Vandivert's photographs of the garden outside the bunker. Yet these three cans of gasoline would have contained barely enough fuel to set the corpses aflame, and certainly not enough to obliterate the bodies by cremating them to ashes.

With the bunker left in the general disarray as described by O'Donnell and seen in Vandivert's photographs, there is no indication whatsoever of a bloody suicide having taken place in the rooms of the Führerbunker.

US hunt for Hitler begins

Almost immediately after the fall of Berlin, US military intelligence organized a mission to hunt for Hitler. An examination of the declassified papers currently in the National Archives at College Park, Maryland, reveal that US military intelligence from November and December 1945 was on the verge of concluding that Hitler had escaped.

The file, for instance, contains a statement dated Berlin, Nov. 23, 1945, made by Erna Flegel, a registered nurse with the Red Cross, who worked during the Battle for Berlin in the hospital created out of the Reich Chancellery for wounded SS troops. In the last few days before the fall of Berlin, Flegel was in the Führerbunker regularly to draw needed supplies from the first-aid room underground. She claimed in her statement to have seen Hitler, as well as Goebbels and his family, in the last few days. "At the end we were like a big family," she wrote. "We were Germany, and we were going through the end of the Third Reich and of the war, concerning the outcome of which we had hoped, up to the end, for a favorable and tolerable issue." Flegel made it clear that she learned on April 30, 1945, that Hitler was dead. She stated as fact that Hitler's body was burned in the garden of the Reich Chancellery.[78]

Remarkably, US military counter-intelligence attached a transmittal form dated Dec. 1, 1945, sending Flegel's statement to the commanding officer, Headquarters Region III, 970th Counter Intelligence Corps, US Army, in Berlin. The attachment noted, "The writer of this document implies the belief that the two caskets contained the bodies of HITLER and his mistress, BRAUN. No evaluation of this 'belief' can be ventured by this office."[79] That US military intelligence would not vouch for the authenticity of a Red Cross registered nurse's statement that Hitler and Eva Braun were dead was an important statement that they lacked proof. That US military intelligence would discount the nurse's statement suggests a conclusion either that those claiming to be eyewitnesses to Hitler's last days in the Führerbunker had been deceived or were lying outright.

As early as October 1945, a US military field intelligence report clearly stated that family close to Eva Braun were making statements suggesting they had positive and reliable information that Hitler had escaped. A US Counter Intelligence Corps (CIC) report dated Oct. 13, 1945, filed in Becknang, Germany, reported on an interview with Mr. and Mrs. Hans Fegelein, the parents of SS-Gruppenführer

---

[78] "Statements of Erna Flegel, R.N., Red Cross Nurse from the Training School 'Markisches Haus', Scharnhorststrasse 3, Born 1911," found in Record Locator 319, Entry (A1) 134-B, Personal File Name, "Hitler," Boxes 295-297, National Archives and Record Administration, NARA, College Park, Maryland.

[79] "Subject: Transmittal of Information (HITLER, Adolf)," signed Sydney Jurin, Operations Officer, Headquarters US Forces European Theater, Counter Intelligence Corps Detachment 970, Region III, APO 757, Dec. 1, 1945, Found in Record Locator 319, NARA, loc.cit. Capitalization in original.

Hermann Fegelein, a Nazi officer in the Waffen-SS who had married Eva Braun's sister, Gretl Braun, and was a trusted member of Hitler's inner circle. According to the CIC field report, Hans Fegelein told US military intelligence investigators, "I think I can say with certainty that the Führer is alive. I have received word through a special courier." The report goes on to detail the further assertions Hans Fegelein made in the interview:

> "Believe me, the Führer is sure to return."
>
> "I got a message through a special messenger. That was not while the war was still in progress. That was not before the death of the Führer was announced, either; it was later, after the capitulation, after his death had already been announced, that I got this message by special courier. My son hinted that he is with the Führer and that the Führer is still alive."
>
> "Yes, I am positive of it, for my son Hermann sent me a courier after the capitulation."
>
> "Yes, at this time they were still in Germany. The courier told me that Hermann [Fegelein] had said to say, 'The Führer and I are safe and well. Don't worry about me; you will get further word from me, even if it is not for some time.' This man, and SS Strumbannführer, also said that on the day when the Führer, Herman, and Eva Braun left Berlin—I think with [Hans] Bauer, Hitler's pilot—there was a sharp counter-attack in Berlin in order to win a flying strip where they could take off."[80]

---

80 "Subject: Whereabouts of HITLER, his mistress, EVA BRAUN, AND HIS ADJUTANT, Gruppenführer HERMANN FEGELEIN," 307TH Counter Intelligence Corps, Headquarters Seventh Army, Becknang, Germany, Oct. 13, 1945, and the attached "Excerpts from statements made by the Fegeleins to Hirschfeld," Found in Record Locator 319, NARA, loc.cit. Brackets inserted for clarity.

Also remarkable in this report is that official Nazi public reports had announced that Hermann Fegelein—despite his close relation to Hitler as the brother-in-law of Eva Braun—had been shot for desertion on April 28, 1945, two days before Hitler and Eva Braun's supposed dual suicide. According to the official Nazi story, Fegelein had been found in civilian clothes trying to escape Berlin. When he was apprehended by Nazi troops, Hitler was furious at Fegelein's disloyalty and had him executed. Here, US military intelligence, by reporting the above statements of Fegelein's father, was suggesting Fegelein's death might have been staged to cover up the role Fegelein played in helping Hitler and Eva Braun escape.

Walter Werner Hirschfeld, a former German SS officer working for the 307th Counter Intelligence Corps at Headquarters Seventh Army and the military intelligence officer who questioned Hans Fegelein, found the statements hard to believe. Consider the following exchange:

> **Hirschfeld:** "But that all sounds so unreal. Even many SS officers state that the Führer is dead and his body was burned."

> **Hans Fegelein:** "Don't let yourself be taken in by propaganda. They are all trusted and true SS men who have orders to make these statements. Dönitz (Admiral, Chief of Fleet; took over government after death of Hitler was announced) probably got orders to make such statements.

And again:

> **Hans Fegelein:** "When I spoke of a courier before, I was referring to the Scharführer or Oberscharführer [General Hermann] Reincke. The latter left Berlin by plane the night before Berlin fell, bringing

with him the possessions of my son, Hermann. He brought from my son word that my son and the Fürher were safe and sound, and that he, my son, would arrive in Fischhorn (near Zell am See, Austria) the next day."

And again:

Hans Fegelein: "The Strumbannführer of whom I have told you, whose name I did not ask and therefore do not know—in any case he did not belong to my son's staff, nor to the Fürher's staff, for then I surely would have known him—appeared in Fischhorn on the day of the capitulation or the day after, and he told me that the Fürher and my son Herman had traveled or flown out of Berlin."

"According to what the Strumbannführer told me, they fought to clear a place from which the plane could take off. Don't let yourself be taken in by rumors; they are saying that my son was shot on orders of Hitler because he was found running around in civilian clothes. That is nonsense. I know positively that the Fürher would never have done such a thing. Do not be taken in by those other rumors either, which state that the Fürher and Eva Braun poisoned themselves and were burned in the courtyard of the Reich Chancellery. None of that is true.

Hans Fegelein advised US military intelligence, "Keep your eye on South America."[81]

Hirschfeld: "Where in South America could the Fürher be, then; that wouldn't work, they would certainly be recognized."

---

[81]   Ibid. All quotes from Hans Fegelein are from the same source.

Hans Fegelein: "It would work, all right; and they have methods of getting there. There were certainly plenty of submarines available. I think the Japanese also helped. They had once planned to go to Japan.

Hirschfeld: "But now Japan is also defeated."

Hans Fegelein: "Yes, they must have considered that, and decided against it for that reason. Yes, you are right; they are in Argentina."[82]

The documents accompanying the interview with Hans Fegelein make clear that US military intelligence believed he had received the message he described and that Fegelein's account was considered credible.

Intelligence reports: Hitler in Argentina

On September 25, 1945, John V. Lapurke, a special agent in the US Counter Intelligence Corps in Austria, filed a highly credible report that Hitler had escaped to Argentina. The first two points of Lapurke's report explain how the information was developed in Austria:

1. On 25 September 1945, GLOCKEL Walter, Personnel Director of the Steyr Auto Works, Steyr, Oberoesterreich, informed this Office that he met Fredrich VON LEON, a former director of the Mauser Arms Works, Berlin, Germany, on 20 September 1945 in Steyr, Bezirk Stery. VON LEON told GLOCKEL that he had heard from a friend of his in Berlin

---

[82]   Ibid.

that ADOLF HITLER is now a guest of one EICH-HORN, living on a farm called LA FALDA, in Argentina. HITLER's host, Señor EICHHORN is an Argentinian of German Descent and is an ardent admirer of Nazi philosophy. EICHHORN is alleged to be an intimate friend of HITLER.

2. According to VON LEON's story, ADOLF HITLER reached Argentina by a German submarine and while on route to Argentina, a famous plastic surgeon remolded HITLER's facial features.[83]

As we shall learn in Chapter Five, Walter and Ida Bonfert Eichhorn were long-standing friends of Adolf Hitler, dating back to 1923 and the famous Beer Hall Putsch in Munich, Germany, that ended with Hitler being arrested and charged for high treason, with his conviction resulting in 264 days of incarceration in Landsberg Prison, where he wrote his famous autobiographical polemic *Mein Kampf*. After Hitler ascended to be Chancellor of Germany in 1933, the Eichhorns, when visiting Germany from Argentina, were frequently honored by Hitler as lunch guests. The intimacy of the friendship is evidenced by the frequently told story that the Eichhorns opened their checkbook to Hitler as he struggled through the criminal process following the failed Hitler-led Nazi insurrection in 1923.

At the end of World War II, the FBI joined US military intelligence in the search for Hitler. The FBI website, in declassifying the FBI records in "the vault" regarding

---

[83]   John V. Lapurke, Special Agent, Counterintelligence Corps, 430 DET., US Forces, Oberoesterreich Section, APO 777, "SUBJECT: Possible location of ADOLF HITLER," Sept. 25, 1945, found in Record Locator 319, NARA, loc.cit. Capitalization in original.

Hitler, notes: "In the aftermath of Germany's surrender in 1945, western Allied forces suspected that Hitler had committed suicide but did not immediately find evidence of his death. At the time, it was feared that Hitler may have escaped in the closing days of the war, and searches were made to determine whether he was still alive. FBI files indicate that the Bureau investigated some of the rumors of Hitler's survival."[84]

A letter from FBI Director J. Edgar Hoover to the American Embassy in Buenos Aires, Argentina, dated Nov. 13, 1945, makes it clear that the FBI had credible information that Hitler had escaped to Argentina with the help of Walter and Ida Bonfert Eichhorn. Hoover's letter began by disclosing that the Strategic Services Unit of the War Department reported to the FBI on Oct. 23, 1945, information concerning the possibility of a "Hitler Hide-out" in Argentina. Hoover's letter detailed the following points from the Strategic Services Unit investigation:

> One Mrs. Eichhorn, reported to be a reputable member of Argentinian society and the proprietor of the largest spa hotel in La Falda, Argentina, made the following observations:
>
> a. That even before the Nazi Party was founded, she made available to Goebbels her entire bank account which, at the time, amounted approximately to thirty thousand marks, which money was to be used for propaganda purposes;
>
> b. That she and her family had been enthusiastic supporters of Adolf Hitler since the Nazi Party was founded;

---

[84]   Federal Bureau of Investigation, FBI Records: "The Vault," Adolf Hitler, http://vault.fbi.gov/adolf-hitler.

c. That this voluntary support of the Nazi Party was never forgotten by Hitler and that during the years after he came into power her friendship with Hitler became so close that she and members of her family lived with Hitler in the same hotel on the occasion of their annual visit to Germany;

d. That if Hitler should at any time get into difficulty wherein it was necessary for him to find a safe retreat, he would find such safe retreat at her hotel (La Falda) where they had already made the necessary preparations.[85]

The highly specific nature of the intelligence information presented here and the fact that the letter was authored by J. Edgar Hoover himself attests to the credibility the FBI gave the report. The general impression is that while the FBI could not prove Hitler was in Argentina, J. Edgar Hoover wanted to put the US Embassy in Buenos Aires on alert because the FBI suspected he was in Argentina and wanted the US Embassy personnel in Buenos Aires to know where to look to find him. Hoover's letter proves the FBI had taken the tip about Walter and Ida Bonfert Eichhorn seriously enough to investigate their background and alert the US Embassy in Buenos Aires to be on the watch for these two particular Argentinian citizens. Hoover, typically very cautious, would surely only write a letter like this if he believed the information conveyed was of sufficient seriousness that he had no choice

---

[85] Letter from John Edgar Hoover, Director, Federal Bureau of Investigation, addressed to the American Embassy in Buenos Aires, Argentina, "Subject: Hitler Hideout in Argentina," dated Nov. 13, 1945, found in FBI Records: "The Vault," Adolf Hitler, vault.fbi.gov/adolf-hitler, at http://vault.fbi.gov/adolf-hitler/adolf-hitler-part-01-of-04/view.

but to hand off the lead to the appropriate US officials in a position to take action.

Eisenhower, "Hitler escaped"

On Monday, October 8, 1945, the US military newspaper *The Stars and Stripes* published a shocking statement by General Dwight D. Eisenhower, then the Supreme Commander of the Allied Forces. The short piece, published in a separate box buried in the middle of a report on pending war crime charges to be brought against Nazi Rudolph Hess and baseball scores from the United States, ran with a headline, "Ike Believes Hitler Lives." The short piece was datelined from London on October 7, 1945. It read: "There is 'reason to believe' that Hitler may still be alive, according to a remark made by Gen. Eisenhower to Dutch newspapermen. The general's statement reversed his previous opinion that Hitler was dead."[86]

The evidence is that US military intelligence in the Counter Intelligence Corps, the FBI, and even the top commander of the US military in Europe, Dwight Eisenhower, all had reason to doubt the official story that Hitler and Eva Braun had died in the Führerbunker on April 30, 1945. Still, the cover-up story that Hitler and Eva Braun died in Berlin ultimately gained acceptance to the point where today the story is the only politically correct version of Hitler's demise not derided by professional historians. How did Trevor-Roper's account become authoritative, despite the obvious inconsistencies between the various eyewitness accounts we saw amply documented in the last chapter?

---

[86] "Ike Believes Hitler Lives," *The Stars and Stripes*, Oct. 8, 1945, p. 8.

Trevor-Roper's "facts"

Among the declassified US military intelligence papers on file at the National Archives are a handwritten and typed version of Trevor-Roper's narrative summarized by Major Edward L. Saxe, who is identified as "Chief, GSC," in the US Army General Services Center, in Germany. It appears Saxe was tasked with preparing for comment and approval Trevor-Roper's major findings before he completed his manuscript, leading to the publication of his book, *The Last Days of Hitler*, in 1947. Saxe's memo is dated October 9, 1945, representing a time span of only eight days after the US Army first issued orders asking for US military yet in the field in Germany to cooperate with Trevor-Roper's investigation.

In the author's preface to the first 1947 publication of his book, Trevor-Roper notes that the idea for his investigation dated to September 1945, when General Dick White, at that time the commander of British military intelligence, invited Trevor-Roper to undertake the study.[87] Saxe's draft of Trevor-Roper's proposed findings, dated October 9, 1945, suggests Trevor-Roper took less than a month to complete a study in which questions have remained open even to today. In this short time between some unspecified date in September 1945, when Trevor-Roper accepted the assignment, and October 9, 1945, when Saxe could write a memo summarizing Trevor-Roper's conclusions, we are to believe Trevor-Roper went into the field to locate eyewitnesses, conducted his interviews, and had enough time to draw conclusions. The hastiness of Trevor-Roper's study suggests the main points of his conclusion could possibly have been derived even before he accepted the assignment.

---

[87]   H. R. Trevor-Roper, *The Last Days of Hitler,* op.cit., "Author's Preface," dated Christ Church, Oxford, Oct. 25, 1946.

The first sentence of Saxe's summary makes it clear that Trevor-Roper's major conclusions were carved in stone after only three weeks. Saxe wrote:

> A detailed investigation into the circumstances surrounding the death of Adolf Hitler has been conducted by Major Trevor-Roper, acting on behalf of the Counter Intelligence War Room and British Army of the Rhine and assisted by this Division. This investigation, which has been underway for three weeks, has included examination of practically all evidence available in the US, British, and French Zones of Occupation.[88]

As noted in the previous chapter, Trevor-Roper's investigation had to have been shortened when he realized the Russians would not allow him to question the Führerbunker eyewitnesses in prison in Moscow, and the Americans appeared willing to share with him only written transcripts of the interviews US military intelligence had conducted with the Führerbunker eyewitnesses in US captivity. Saxe acknowledged in his second point that Trevor-Roper's investigation "as a whole is not yet considered to be complete, owing to the difficulties involved in locating all available witnesses." Yet, in the next sentence, Saxe asserts that Trevor-Roper has carefully cross-examined several unnamed "material witnesses," permitting him to have established "sufficiently" what were listed as the following facts. Among those facts were:

- That on the night of 29 April, Hitler decided to commit suicide on the following day. He took

---

[88] Edward L. Saxe, Major, GSC, Chief, Operations Section, "SUBJECT: Circumstances Surrounding the Death of Adolf Hitler," Oct. 9, 1945, found in Record Locator 319, NARA, loc.cit.

leave of his servants at 0230 hours on 30 April and preparations were made for the destruction of his body and that of Eva Braun on the morning of 30 April.

- That on 30 April at 1430 hours Hitler took leave of his personal staff in the bunker and almost immediately afterwards shot himself while in his private room. Eva Braun committed suicide at the same time, probably by poisoning.

- That the bodies were then carried out of the bunker and burned, as arranged, in the garden.

As a key eyewitness, Saxe cited Hitler's chauffeur, Erich Kempka, whose testimony we previously discussed as being highly suspect. Saxe admits the stories Trevor-Roper was relying upon being accurate eyewitness testimony were "all fragmentary". But Sax insists these fragmentary stories "form a consistent pattern which has been checked by detailed cross-examination." Saxe does not consider the possibility that the witnesses were giving fragmentary accounts because they were relating a cover story made up by the witnesses to hide the truth that Hitler had escaped. In concluding, Saxe admitted the bodies of Hitler and Eva Braun "have not, of course, been identified." Yet he asserted, "It is to be noted that certain alternative stories which have gained currency since the fall of Berlin have been examined and have been found to rest on no valid evidence."

Evidently Trevor-Roper's investigation was not sufficient to impress Eisenhower that Hitler was dead. The report in *The Stars and Stripes* that Eisenhower had changed his mind to think Hitler had escaped and was alive was published the day before Saxe sat down to type his report of Trevor-Roper's conclusions to the contrary. Still, in the final analysis, the pressure to be politically correct weighed on Eisenhower as he was preparing to enter politics. In his 1948 book on World War II, *Crusade in Europe*, Eisenhower portrayed Hitler's demise as a suicide, commenting: "Hitler had committed suicide and the tattered mantle of his authority had fallen to Admiral Doenitz."[89]

Hitler killed by artillery fire?

The declassified US military intelligence documents in the National Archives make clear that a second story of how Hitler died was prepared and ready for use, just in case the inconsistencies in eyewitness testimony and the lack of a corpse or any other physical evidence Hitler committed suicide began to cause suspicion.

On September 10, 1945, Dr. Karlheinz Spaeth provided a sworn and signed statement to First Lieutenant Dennison G. Stevens of the US Summary Military Government Court in Germany about how he attended Hitler after he had been mortally wounded by Russian artillery fire. Spaeth swore to the following:

> During the last months of the war I was the battalion doctor with the 2nd Battalion, 23 Regt. 9th Parachute Division. Our unit was engaged in battle in and around Berlin (area of Kuestrin). On the 1st of May I had established a collecting station in the cellar of the Landwehrkasino right across from the Bunker at the Zoo. Along about 3 o'clock in the afternoon I was informed that Hitler was in our sector. I left

---

[89] Dwight D. Eisenhower, *Crusade in Europe* (Garden City, New York: Doubleday & Company, Inc., 1948), p. 424.

the cellar and went into the street in order to see
him, or get a look at him. The commander of the
battalion, Oberstleutnant Graf von Raiffenstein,
received a report from Lt. Kurt Uhlik, who was leading Company 5, that there was continuous artillery
and trench mortar fire outside in front of the tank
barricade, which was stationed in the subterranean
passage to the zoo.

Spaeth continued the narrative, pointing out that Hitler
ignored the fact that it would be dangerous to approach
the tank barrier.

Hitler ignored the warning and walked to the dangerous spot, and was, according to general opinion,
wounded together with a number of SS leaders. I saw
that there was considerable excitement and hubbub
at the tank barricade. I was called shortly thereaf-
ter and saw the following: Hitler was lowered to the
floor in cover. A shell fragment, about 10 cm long
and 8 to 10 mm wide had pierced the uniform, went
through his chest, and entered the lungs on both
sides. It was no use to do anything. I took a few first
aid bandages, which I had with me, and bandaged
him. During this time Hitler groaned continuously.
He was not fully conscious. To relieve his pains, I
went back to my collecting station to get some mor-
phine, and gave him a double strength injection.

The Russian shelling made it impossible to move Hitler
to a safe shelter, Spaeth described, making it clear he knew
Hitler would die.

After I had pronounced the Führer dead, and
informed the SS leaders of this fact, I was released
and went back to my work. I had one of the soldiers

take a sheet to the spot where Hitler had died. The soldier came back with the sheet, and informed me he had been told the sheet was not needed, as the corpse would be destroyed. According to the reports of two other soldiers, which were handed to me about two hours later, the body of Hitler had been blown into the air by the surviving SS leaders with two three-kilogram charges. Whether or not this is so, I cannot say, because the building was hit continuously by artillery fire, and one detonation could not be distinguished from another.[90]

Whether this version of Hitler's death failed to advance because it was considered incredible, too fantastic to be believed, or because the suicide story had more depth and witnesses, is unknown. Clearly, it wasn't possible for both versions of Hitler's death to be true. Spaeth's signed deposition was produced in both German and English versions and accompanied by a hand-drawn diagram where Spaeth indicated precisely where he was claiming Hitler had been hit by the artillery fire. Spaeth concluded his deposition by making clear the Soviet army had held him captive at the Prisoner of War Hospital at Potsdam. "During my stay in the hospital, myself, the medical personnel, and other officers were interviewed by a Russian captain," Spaeth concluded his deposition. "We stated at the time that Hitler died in action, [I] made a sketch and reported the same as above stated."[91]

---

[90] Second Lieutenant QMC Lyons T. Carr, Allied Expiditionary Force, Military Government, Illertissen, Bavaria, "Subject: Hitler's Death," Sept. 10, 1945. Attached was a deposition in German, signed by Dr. Spaeth, "who was the doctor in attendance on Hitler when he died," plus an English translation of the deposition.

[91] Ibid. Bracket added for clarity.

The Hitler marriage and will

One additional factor may have influenced the choice of the suicide story as the preferred version of Hitler's death. The eyewitnesses in the Führerbunker described how Hitler in the last days took two steps that indicated he was preparing to die: First, he signed his last will and testament, and second, he married Eva Braun, but only after Eva Braun agreed to die with him in Berlin. That the most notorious mass murderer at the end of his life should entertain such mundane sentiments as the desire to tie up loose ends of his genocidal and criminally immoral life by writing a will and marrying his mistress seems decidedly out of character. Still, the point of the story appears to be to set the Hitler and Eva Braun double-suicide story in an emotional context. Less suspicious critics would therefore be led along to think the double-suicide had been preceded by Hitler and Eva Braun taking end-of-life steps to somehow legitimize a longtime love relationship that had been hidden from the general awareness of the German people.

If the marriage ceremony and the last will and testament were fabricated, very possibly the goal was to add an element of sentimentality to Hitler's last days in order to make his suicide more believable to ordinary citizens worldwide. Somehow, the Nazi propagandist positioning of Hitler for public consumption could easily have calculated that having Hitler marry Eva Braun would achieve the same emotional impact upon the German people as had been accomplished before the war with the many photographs taken showing Hitler greeting children with a smile or portraying him as a loving master of his various German shepherd dogs. A skillful propagandist such as Goebbels would have appreciated the message subtly communicated by the contrivance: Hitler may have caused the deaths of more than fifty million in World War II, but he liked children and was kind to his dogs, so in the end he also married the woman he loved.

On May 16, 1945, Lieutenant General Lucien K. Truscott, commanding the Third US Army and the Eastern Military District, announced that, after a long search, Third Army intelligence officers had found a signed copy of Hitler's will, witnessed by Joseph Goebbels, Martin Bormann, Hans Krebs, and Wilhelm Burgdorf. Additionally found was an original marriage license between Hitler and Eva Braun, witnessed by Goebbels and Bormann. In making the announcement, Truscott noted that Hitler's will expressed "Hitler's wish that he and Eva Braun, whom he married when she volunteered to share his fate in the besieged Berlin, should be cremated 'immediately at the place where I have done the greatest part of my work during the twelve years service for my people.'" Truscott noted Hitler's reference was apparently to the Reich Chancellery. Truscott allowed the US military to make public that part of Hitler's will in which he blamed Jews for the start of World War II. In the last will and testament, Hitler raved: "It is not true that I or anybody else in Germany wanted the war in the year 1939. It was desired and provoked entirely by those international statesman who were either of Jewish origin or who worked in the Jewish interests."

There is considerable evidence that the Hitler will was forged and the marriage ceremony with Eva Braun never happened. Surgeon Hugh Thomas in his 1995 book, *The Murder of Adolf Hitler*, noted the lack of independent verification that Hitler's marriage to Eva Braun ever took place. "There has been surprisingly little argument about Hitler's marriage to Eva Braun, allegedly carried out by Walter Wagner, *gauleiter* of Berlin, on 29 April, in the map room in the Bunker, in front of Bormann and Goebbels as witnesses," he wrote. "This paucity of argument is despite the claims of several, including Hanna Reitsch and General Robert Ritter von Greim, that the marriage ever took place."[92] Hanna Reitsch was a renowned German aviatrix who was awarded the Iron Cross for her heroism flying in World War II. She is known to have made a daring landing in Berlin and visited Hitler in the Führerbunker, and to have met with him shortly before the fall of Berlin. General Robert Ritter von Greim, a German Field Marshal and army pilot who was reputedly Reitsch's lover, was the passenger accompanying Reitsch in the daring Berlin landing. Supposedly, after visiting with Reitsch and Ritter von Greim, Hitler ordered Reitsch to fly herself and Greim out of Berlin, a feat accomplished by taking off from a Tiergarten strip near the Brandenburg Gate cleared for that purpose. Reitsch narrowly managed as the Soviet Third Shock Army advanced. Russian soldiers watching Reitsch's plane lift off from Berlin were at the time convinced they had just witnessed Hitler's escape.

Hugh Thomas is equally skeptical over the authenticity of Hitler's last will and testament. He was especially critical that Trevor-Roper had accepted the document as authentic based on expert scrutiny of the signature and the testimony of Frau Gertruad Junge, Hitler's secretary, who had typed the documents. "Since the fiasco of the

---

[92] Hugh Thomas, *The Murder of Adolf Hitler*, op.cit., p. 99.

Hitler Diaries, the public has become skeptical about the abilities of handwriting experts and historians, but there are pointers which suggest that it was Goebbels who either invented, dictated or altered the final version of the will, as the language is so similar to his own," Hugh Thomas wrote. "The signature [Hitler's]—no more than a squiggle—could have been genuine, a good forgery or even a bad forgery—there was, and is, no scientific way of telling."[93]

---

[93]   Ibid., p. 100.

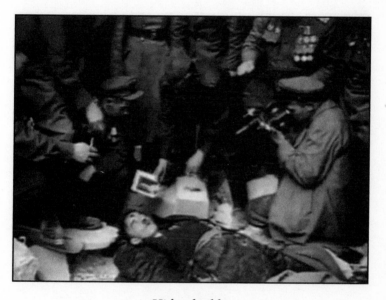

Hitler double
In the garden outside the Führerbunker
Berlin, May 2, 1945
Soviet army propaganda film, 1945

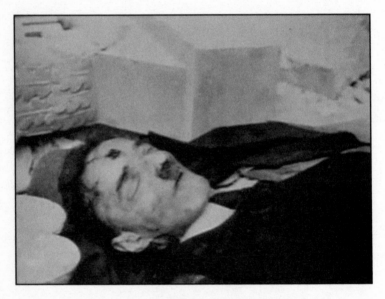

Hitler double, close-up view
In the garden outside the Führerbunker
Berlin, May 2, 1945
Soviet army propaganda film, 1945

Hitler double
In the garden outside the Führerbunker
Berlin, May 2, 1945
Soviet army propaganda film, 1945

Hitler double
In the garden outside the Führerbunker
Berlin, May 2, 1945
Soviet army propaganda film, 1945

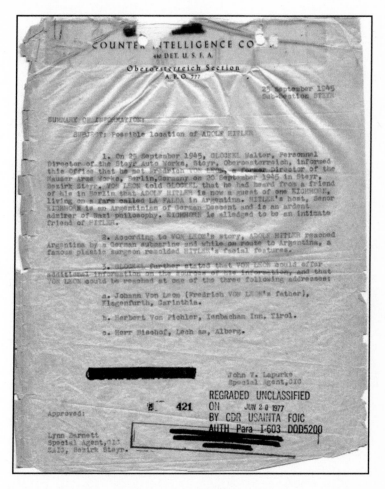

COUNTER INTELLIGENCE CO___
440 DET. U. S. F. A.
Oberoesterreich Section
A. P. O. 777

25 September 1945
Sub-Section STEYR

SUMMARY OF INFORMATION:

SUBJECT: Possible location of ADOLF HITLER

1. On 25 September 1945, GLOCKEL Walter, Personnel Director of the Steyr Auto Works, Steyr, Oberoesterreich, informed this Office that he met Friedrich VON LEON, a former Director of the Mauser Arms Works, Berlin, Germany on 20 September 1945 in Steyr, Bezirk Steyr. VON LEON told GLOCKEL that he had heard from a friend of his in Berlin that ADOLF HITLER is now a guest of one EICHHORN, living on a farm called LA FALDA in Argentina. HITLER's host, Senor EICHHORN is an Argentinian of German Descent and is an ardent admirer of Nazi philosophy. EICHHORN is alledged to be an intimate friend of HITLER.

2. According to VON LEON's story, ADOLF HITLER reached Argentina by a German submarine and while on route to Argentina, a famous plastic surgeon resolded HITLER's facial features.

3. GLOCKEL further stated that VON LEON could offer additional information on the sources of his information, and that VON LEON could be reached at one of the three following addresses:

a. Johann Von Leon (Fredrich VON LEON's father), Klagenfurth, Carinthia.

b. Herbert Von Pichler, Iambacham Inn, Tirol.

c. Herr Bischof, Lech am, Alberg.

John V. Lapurke
Special Agent, CIC

REGRADED UNCLASSIFIED
ON   JUN 20 1977
BY CDR USAINTA FOIC
AUTH Para 1-603 DOD5200

Approved:

E   421

Lynn Barnett
Special Agent, CIC
SAIC, Bezirk Steyr.

Declassified US Army Counter Intelligence Corps report detailing information Hitler had escaped to Argentina
September 25, 1945.

Source: Record Locator 319, Entry (A1) 134-B,
Personal File Name, "Hitler," Boxes 295-297,
National Archives and Record Administration, NARA,
College Park, Maryland.

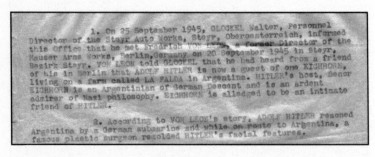

1. On 25 September 1945, GLOCKEL Walter, Personnel Director of the Steyr Auto Works, Steyr, Oberoesterreich, informed this office that he met Friedrich VON LEON, a former Director of the Mauser Arms Works, Berlin,Germany on 20 September 1945 in Steyr, Bezirk Steyr. VON LEON told GLOCKEL that he had heard from a friend of his in Berlin that ADOLF HITLER is now a guest of one EICHHORN, living on a farm called LA FALDA in Argentina. HITLER's host, Senor EICHHORN is an Argentinian of German Descent and is an ardent admirer of Nazi philosophy. EICHHORN is alledged to be an intimate friend of HITLER.

2. According to VON LEON's story, ADOLF HITLER reached Argentina by a German submarine and while on route to Argentina, a famous plastic surgeon remolded HITLER's facial features.

Detailed view:
Declassified US Army Counter Intelligence Corps report detailing information Hitler had escaped to Argentina
September 25, 1945.

Source: Record Locator 319, Entry (A1) 134-B,
Personal File Name, "Hitler," Boxes 295-297,
National Archives and Record Administration, NARA,
College Park, Maryland.

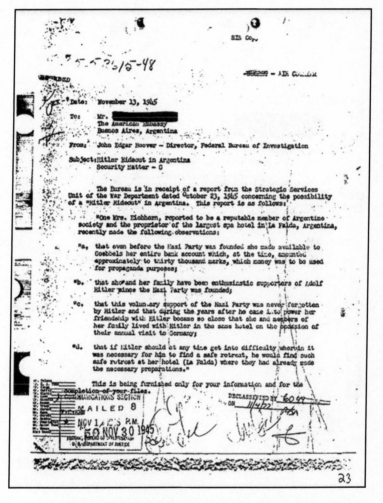

RECORDED

Date: November 13, 1945

To: Mr. ▓▓▓▓▓▓▓
The American Embassy
Buenos Aires, Argentina

From: John Edgar Hoover — Director, Federal Bureau of Investigation

Subject: Hitler Hideout in Argentina
Security Matter - G

The Bureau is in receipt of a report from the Strategic Services Unit of the War Department dated October 23, 1945 concerning the possibility of a "Hitler Hideout" in Argentina. This report is as follows:

"One Mrs. Eichhorn, reported to be a reputable member of Argentine society and the proprietor of the largest spa hotel in La Falda, Argentina, recently made the following observations:

"a. that even before the Nazi Party was founded she made available to Goebbels her entire bank account which, at the time, amounted approximately to thirty thousand marks, which money was to be used for propaganda purposes;

"b. that she and her family have been enthusiastic supporters of Adolf Hitler since the Nazi Party was founded;

"c. that this voluntary support of the Nazi Party was never forgotten by Hitler and that during the years after he came into power her friendship with Hitler became so close that she and members of her family lived with Hitler in the same hotel on the occasion of their annual visit to Germany;

"d. that if Hitler should at any time get into difficulty wherein it was necessary for him to find a safe retreat, he would find such safe retreat at her hotel (La Falda) where they had already made the necessary preparations."

This is being furnished only for your information and for the completion of your files.

COMMUNICATIONS SECTION
MAILED 8
NOV 1 ▓▓ P.M.
50 NOV 30 1945
FEDERAL BUREAU OF INVESTIGATION
U.S. DEPARTMENT OF JUSTICE

DECLASSIFIED BY 60 69
ON 11/4/72

23

Letter from John Edgar Hoover, Director, Federal Bureau
of Investigation, addressed to the American
Embassy in Buenos Aires, Argentina
"Subject: Hitler Hideout in Argentina,"
dated November 13, 1945, p. 1.

Source: FBI Records: "The Vault," Adolf Hitler, Part 1,
vault.fbi.gov/adolf-hitler.

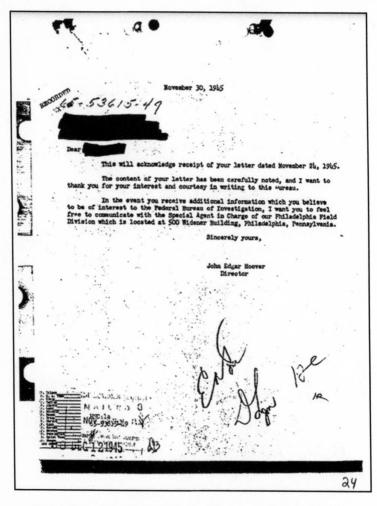

November 30, 1945

RECORDED
65 - 53615 - 49

Dear ▓▓▓▓▓

This will acknowledge receipt of your letter dated November 24, 1945.

The content of your letter has been carefully noted, and I want to thank you for your interest and courtesy in writing to this Bureau.

In the event you receive additional information which you believe to be of interest to the Federal Bureau of Investigation, I want you to feel free to communicate with the Special Agent in Charge of our Philadelphia Field Division which is located at 500 Widener Building, Philadelphia, Pennsylvania.

Sincerely yours,

John Edgar Hoover
Director

MAILED 3
NOV 30 1945

DEC 12 1945

24

Letter from John Edgar Hoover, Director, Federal Bureau of Investigation, addressed to the American Embassy in Buenos Aires, Argentina "Subject: Hitler Hideout in Argentina," dated November 13, 1945, p. 2.

Source: FBI Records: "The Vault," Adolf Hitler, Part 1 vault.fbi.gov/adolf-hitler.

"One Mrs. Eichhorn, reported to be a reputable member of Argentine society and the proprietor of the largest spa hotel in La Falda, Argentina, recently made the following observations:

"a. that even before the Nazi Party was founded she made available to Goebbels her entire bank account which, at the time, amounted approximately to thirty thousand marks, which money was to be used for propaganda purposes;

"b. that she and her family have been enthusiastic supporters of Adolf Hitler since the Nazi Party was founded;

"c. that this voluntary support of the Nazi Party was never forgotten by Hitler and that during the years after he came into power her friendship with Hitler became so close that she and members of her family lived with Hitler in the same hotel on the occasion of their annual visit to Germany;

"d. that if Hitler should at any time get into difficulty wherein it was necessary for him to find a safe retreat, he would find such safe retreat at her hotel (La Falda) where they had already made the necessary preparations."

Detailed view:
Letter from John Edgar Hoover, Director, Federal Bureau of Investigation, addressed to the American Embassy in Buenos Aires, Argentina "Subject: Hitler Hideout in Argentina," dated November 13, 1945, p. 3.

Source: FBI Records: "The Vault," Adolf Hitler, Part 1, vault.fbi.gov/adolf-hitler.

Full-page view:
"Ike Believes Hitler Lives," *The Stars and Stripes*,
Monday, October 8, 1945, p. 8

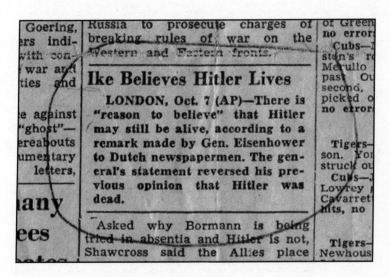

Detailed view:
"Ike Believes Hitler Lives," *The Stars and Stripes*,
Monday, October 8, 1945, p. 8

9 October 1945

MEMORANDUM TO: Chief, CIB

SUBJECT: Circumstances Surrounding the Death of Adolf Hitler.

1. A detailed investigation into the circumstances surrounding the death of Adolf Hitler has been conducted by Major Trevor-Roper, acting in behalf of the Counter Intelligence War Room and British Army of the Rhine and assisted by this Division. This investigation, which has been underway for three weeks, has included examination of practically all evidence available in the U.S., British and French Zones of Occupation.

2. The investigation as a whole is not yet considered to be complete owing to the difficulties involved in locating all available witnesses. A careful cross examination of several material witnesses has, however, sufficiently established the following facts:

    a. That Hitler definitely decided on 22 April not to leave Berlin, but to stay and, if the city fell, to die there. In the latter event, his body was to be destroyed and plans for the complete destruction of his body were made.

    b. That on the night of 29 April, Hitler decided to commit suicide on the following day. He took leave of his servants at 0230 on 30 April and preparations for the destruction of his body and that of Eva Braun were made on the morning of 30 April.

    c. That on 30 April at 1430 Hitler took leave of his personal staff in the bunker and almost immediately afterwards shot himself while in his private room. Eva Braun committed suicide at the same time, probably by poisoning.

    d. That the bodies were then carried out of the bunker and burned, as arranged, in the garden.

3. The witnesses so far examined fall into the following independent groups:

    a. Several politicians, officials and officers who were acquainted with Hitler's intentions and who had all left the bunker by 29 April, including Speer, Berger (Chief of SS Hauptamt), Gen. Koller (Luftwaffe), Himmler's adjutants and advisers, including Schellenberg and Dr. Gebhart (Himmler's doctor and adviser).

    b. A woman who was casually present at the leave taking of 0230, 30 April and who was not known to any other witnesses.

    c. Hitler's chauffeur, Kempka, who obtained the gasoline on the morning of 30 April and helped to carry the bodies of Hitler and Braun to the point where they were burned, which procedure he witnessed.

415

Edward L. Saxe, Major, GSC, Chief, Operations Section
"SUBJECT: Circumstances Surrounding
the Death of Adolf Hitler"
October 9, 1945, p. 1.

Source: Record Locator 319, Entry (A1) 134-B,
Personal File Name, "Hitler," Boxes 295-297,
National Archives and Record Administration, NARA,
College Park, Maryland.

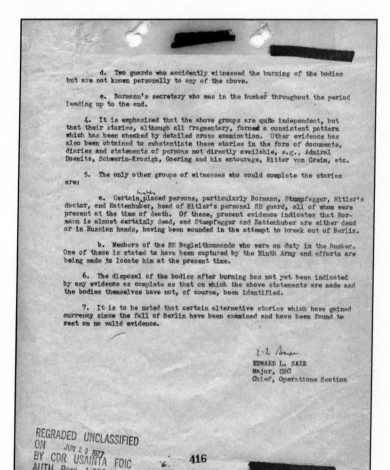

    d. Two guards who accidently witnessed the burning of the bodies but are not known personally to any of the above.

    e. Bormann's secretary who was in the bunker throughout the period leading up to the end.

    4. It is emphasized that the above groups are quite independent, but that their stories, although all fragmentary, formed a consistent pattern which has been checked by detailed cross examination. Other evidence has also been obtained to substantiate these stories in the form of documents, diaries and statements of persons not directly available, e.g., Admiral Doenitz, Schwerin-Krosigk, Goering and his entourage, Ritter von Greim, etc.

    5. The only other groups of witnesses who could complete the stories are:

    a. Certain placed persons, particularly Bormann, Stumpfegger, Hitler's doctor, and Rattenhuber, head of Hitler's personal SD guard, all of whom were present at the time of death. Of these, present evidence indicates that Bormann is almost certainly dead, and Stumpfegger and Rattenhuber are either dead or in Russian hands, having been wounded in the attempt to break out of Berlin.

    b. Members of the SS Begleitkommando who were on duty in the Bunker. One of these is stated to have been captured by the Ninth Army and efforts are being made to locate him at the present time.

    6. The disposal of the bodies after burning has not yet been indicated by any evidence as complete as that on which the above statements are made and the bodies themselves have not, of course, been identified.

    7. It is to be noted that certain alternative stories which have gained currency since the fall of Berlin have been examined and have been found to rest on no valid evidence.

EDWARD L. SAXE
Major, GSC
Chief, Operations Section

Edward L. Saxe, Major, GSC, Chief, Operations Section
"SUBJECT: Circumstances Surrounding
the Death of Adolf Hitler"
October 9, 1945, p. 1.

Source: Record Locator 319, Entry (A1) 134-B,
Personal File Name, "Hitler," Boxes 295-297,
National Archives and Record Administration, NARA,
College Park, Maryland.

1. A detailed investigation into the circumstances surrounding the death of Adolf Hitler has been conducted by Major Trevor-Roper, acting in behalf of the Counter Intelligence War Room and British Army of the Rhine and assisted by this Division. This investigation, which has been underway for three weeks, has included examination of practically all evidence available in the U.S., British and French Zones of Occupation.

2. The investigation as a whole is not yet considered to be complete owing to the difficulties involved in locating all available witnesses. A careful cross examination of several material witnesses has, however, sufficiently established the following facts:

a. That Hitler definitely decided on 22 April not to leave Berlin, but to stay and, if the city fell, to die there. In the latter event, his body was to be destroyed and plans for the complete destruction of his body were made.

b. That on the night of 29 April, Hitler decided to commit suicide on the following day. He took leave of his servants at 0230 on 30 April and preparations for the destruction of his body and that of Eva Braun were made on the morning of 30 April.

c. That on 30 April at 1430 Hitler took leave of his personal staff in the bunker and almost immediately afterwards shot himself while in his private room. Eva Braun committed suicide at the same time, probably by poisoning.

d. That the bodies were then carried out of the bunker and burned, as arranged, in the garden.

Detailed view:
Edward L. Saxe, Major, GSC, Chief, Operations Section
"SUBJECT: Circumstances Surrounding
the Death of Adolf Hitler"
October 9, 1945, p. 1.

Source: Record Locator 319, Entry (A1) 134-B,
Personal File Name, "Hitler," Boxes 295-297,
National Archives and Record Administration, NARA,
College Park, Maryland.

German U-Boat U-530 arrives, Mar del Plata, Argentina,
July 10, 1945
Ahora, July 14, 1945
Buenos Aires, Argentina

Source: Record Locator 38, OP162, Interrogations and
Documents from U-Boats 1945-1945, Box 23,
National Archives and Record Administration, NARA,
College Park, Maryland.

COPY No. _____
(Use Reveal Device only)

MILITARY INTELLIGENCE DIVISION W. D. G. S.

MILITARY ATTACHE REPORT   Argentina

(Country reported on)

Subject German Submarine Surrenders to Argentine Navy   I.G. No. 0501.0207
(Title of newspaper item)   3123.0404

From M. A. Argentina   Report No. R-509-45   Date 18 July 1945

Source and degree of reliability:

Confidential	Rating: As indicated

SUMMARY.—Here enter careful summary of report, containing substance concisely stated; include important facts, names, places, dates, etc.

1. (A-1) At 7.30 am on 10 July 1945, the 700-ton 50-meter German submarine U-530 surfaced in the harbor at Mar del Plata and surrendered to the Argentine Navy. The U-530 was commanded by 25-year old Captain Otto WERMUTH and carried a crew of 54 men. The oldest member of the crew was a 45-year old warrant officer, one of the engineers was 32 years old, and the rest of the crew averaged 22 years of age, with the youngest 19. The Argentine Ministry of Marine issued a communiqué the evening of 11 July, stating that interrogation of the crew and inspection of the submarine proved that:

    a. The U-530 had nothing to do with the sinking of the Brazilian cruiser "Bahia".

    b. She did not carry any German politicians or military officials.

    c. No persons were landed on the Argentine coast prior to the surrender.

    d. All personnel aboard were bona fide crew members.

On 16 July, the officers and crew were taken under guard to Martín García, a small detention island in the Rio de la Plata. Details on crew members and their fingerprints have been or will be turned over to United States and British authorities. A special committee appointed by the Ministry of Foreign Affairs recommended on 16 July that the submarine and crew be placed at the disposal of the United States and British authorities. The question was discussed in a Cabinet meeting held on 17 July and it was decreed that both submarines and crew with reports and findings of Argentine naval authorities would be turned over to United States and British authorities.

2. (B-3) Local newspapermen have reported the following:

Distribution by originator   MIS -- Chancery

Routing space below for use in M. I. D. The section indicating the distribution will place a check mark in the lower part of the recipient's box in case one copy only is to go to him, or will indicate the number of copies in case more than one should be sent. The message center of the Intelligence Branch will draw a circle around the box of the recipient to which the particular copy is to go.

A&F	AAF	ASF	AC of S G-2	Chief IB	Exec.etc.	Far East	N. Amer.	Air	Disesse.	AIC	FLE R	OSS
U.S. Sec.	CIG	Rec. Sec.	GN I	SEW	GWS	ENG.	OFG	ORD	Sp.	State	QMG	

Enclosures:

Copy of report of Naval Attaché
of 13 July 1945

MIS 283115

CPM 1
MII 2
*Pol 2
Route
Lib
WW 1
W Eur Spc 1
Dir Inf 1
HQA/F 1
ONI 3
State 3
* MIS 1
Pol 1
Route

US Naval Attaché, Military Intelligence Division, "German Submarine Surrenders to Argentine Navy," July 18, 1945, p. 1.

Source: Record Locator 38, OP162, Interrogations and Documents from U-Boats 1945-1945, Box 23, National Archives and Record Administration, NARA, College Park, Maryland.

C O N F I D E N T I A L

Captain WERMUTH has stated that the U-530 left her German home base on 19 February 1945, preyed on shipping along the Norwegian coast until 13 March, and then took up patrol work in the South Atlantic. None of the crew has identification papers, the combat-log is missing. all armament was destroyed or rendered useless, the bow gun and two anti-aircraft guns are missing, and the only ammunition left aboard is in such condition as to be useless. There was plenty of food aboard but very little fuel. The crew was in good condition and very little information of value could be gotten from any of them. The ship's log and instruments were intact and the submarine was fitted with a particularly powerful radio which was in operating condition. The crew of 54 men was 16 men over the normal crew of 38 men for a submarine of that class.

Newsmen have also reported (C-4) the following rumors:

A submarine was sighted by an Argentine Navy transport about the middle of June and was subsequently hunted by Argentine warships. Two men landed near San Julián (Territory of Santa Cruz) about 1 July 1945, coming in a rubber boat and being met by a sailing boat. The submarine refueled from drums hidden under water along the coast at a place marked with three large stones near a tamarisk grove. Another submarine is on the way to Argentina to surrender. The Assistant Chief of the Department of Investigations informed the Federal Police that a submarine was going to surrender some time before the actual surrender took place. Eva BRAUN and Adolf HITLER were landed in the south of Argentina.

3. (B-3) It is said in police circles that the submarine put in at Comodoro Rivadavia before surrendering at Mar del Plata.

4. (B-3) A resident of Coronel Dorrego, Province of Buenos Aires, reported that on or about 22 June 1945 some people landed on the coast near that town from a rubber boat. The landings were discussed by the people of the town but it is not believed that the police were notified.

5. (B-4) On the evening of 9 July, the day before the submarine surrendered, a celebration was held in a private dining room of the Nazi Jousten Hotel to celebrate the arrival of some important Nazis in Argentina. Celebrations were also held in other Nazi meeting places for the same reason. On 17 July, the same source reported that HITLER and five other men had landed (time and place unknown) in a restricted military district far in the south of Argentina. They are said to have come in from the sea in two power boats, flying the Argentine official flag.

6. (A-1) Captain WEBB, United States Naval Attaché, and Commander Lloyd HIRST, British Assistant Naval Attaché, went to Mar del Plata to inspect the submarine and interrogate the crew on 10 July and returned on 11 July. Representatives from their offices and from the office of the Legal Attaché have been in close touch with the case and copy of the Naval Attaché report, dated 13 July 1945, which is the only one we have received to date, is inclosed. Commander HIRST did state that the submarine was in a particularly foul condition and that evidently discipline must have broken down some time before the surrender. He further remarked that the officers and men of the submarine crew were extremely arrogant and that they were receiving excellent and deferential treatment from the Argentine authorities. Captain Julio C. MALLEA, Commanding Officer of the submarine base, is known to have pro-Nazi tendencies and to be married to a daughter of Juan P. RAMOS, well known Nationalist and pro-Nazi.

US Naval Attaché, Military Intelligence Division,
"German Submarine Surrenders to Argentine Navy,"
July 18, 1945, p. 2.

CONFIDENTIAL
CONFIDENTIAL

7. (B-2) At 4 pm on 7 June 1945, an individual unknown to any of the habitués of the port area arrived at the port of Mar del Plata aboard the shark fishing boat "Juncal" and left immediately for Buenos Aires. This man appeared to be from 40 to 45 years of age, 6'6" tall, thin, blond, partly bald, and with a large nose. The "Juncal" is a 17-meter ocean-going fishing boat with a speed of 13 knots and can and does stay at sea from three to four days at a time. She has sleeping space for five and is at sea a great deal, but brings in very few sharks.

(B-2) At 6 pm on 5 July 1945, the ocean-going yacht "San Lorenzo" put in at the port of Mar del Plata with persons aboard who were entirely unknown to the fishermen of the port area.

8. (B-3) A Nazi agent, known to have been in the employ of Pedro ILVESTO, who was considered one of Juan Sigfrido BECKER's right-hand men, was seen in Miramar, south of Mar del Plata, the first week in July. It is unusual for anyone to go to this resort town during the winter unless they have some unusual business in mind.

9. (B-2) At about 3 pm on 17 July 1945, two submarines were sighted some three kilometers off General Lavalle, halfway between BuenosAires and Mar del Plata. Visibility was such that they could not be identified but at 4 pm they were reported to be heading for Mar del Plata escorted by Argentine navy planes. On the morning of 18 July, the Argentine Navy denied that there were any German submarines, other than the U-530, in Argentine waters.

10. The above rumors are being investigated and further reports will be submitted. A careful interrogation of the crew (four of whom have Polish names) by experts will probably furnish the best evidence as to whether or not the sub actually landed passengers.

                                        0105 D. F. GIBBONS
                                             Major, Cavalry
                                             Asst. Military Attaché

Approved and forwarded

A. R. HARRIS
Brig Gen, USA
Military Attaché

DFG/sa

From M/A Argentina   Report N° R-509-45   18 July 1945
        Page N° 3   CONFIDENTIAL

US Naval Attaché, Military Intelligence Division, "German Submarine Surrenders to Argentine Navy," July 18, 1945, p. 3.

Source: Record Locator 38, OP162, Interrogations and Documents from U-Boats 1945-1945, Box 23, National Archives and Record Administration, NARA, College Park, Maryland.

Captain WEHMUTH has stated that the U-530 left her German home base on 19 February 1945, preyed on shipping along the Norwegian coast until 13 March, and then took up patrol work in the South Atlantic. None of the crew has identification papers, the combat-log is missing, all armament was destroyed or rendered useless, the bow gun and two anti-aircraft guns are missing; and the only ammunition left aboard is in such condition as to be useless. There was plenty of food aboard but very little fuel. The crew was in good condition and very little information of value could be gotten from any of them. The ship's log and instruments were intact and the submarine was fitted with a particularly powerful radio which was in operating condition. The crew of 54 men was 16 men over the normal crew of 38 men for a submarine of that class.

Newsmen have also reported (C-4) the following rumors:

A submarine was sighted by an Argentine Navy transport about the middle of June and was subsequently hunted by Argentine warships. Two men landed near San Julián (Territory of Santa Cruz) about 1 July 1945, coming in a rubber boat and being met by a sailing boat. The submarine refueled from drums hidden under water along the coast at a place marked with three large stones near a tamarisk grove. Another submarine is on the way to Argentina to surrender. The Assistant Chief of the Department of Investigations informed the Federal Police that a submarine was going to surrender some time before the actual surrender took place. Eva BRAUN and Adolf HITLER were landed in the south of Argentina.

Detailed view:
US Naval Attaché, Military Intelligence Division,
"German Submarine Surrenders to Argentine Navy,"
July 18, 1945, p. 1.

Source: Record Locator 38, OP162, Interrogations and
Documents from U-Boats 1945-1945, Box 23,
National Archives and Record Administration, NARA,
College Park, Maryland.

Mug shot of Commanding Officer Oberleutnant
(Lieutenant Junior Grade) Otto Wermuth, 25 years old
U-530, Mar del Plata, Argentina, July 12, 1945

Source: Record Locator 38, OP162, Interrogations and
Documents from U-Boats 1945-1945, Box 23,
National Archives and Record Administration, NARA,
College Park, Maryland.

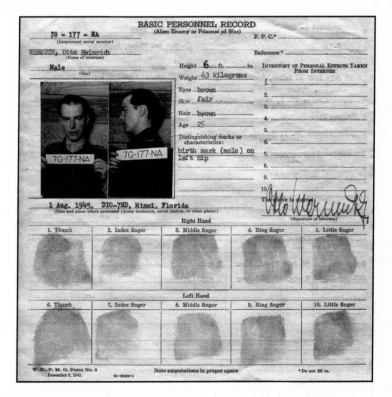

Mug shot of Commanding Officer Oberleutnant
(Lieutenant Junior Grade) Otto Wermuth, 25 years old
U-530, Miami, Florida, August 1945

Source: Record Locator 38, OP162, Interrogations and
Documents from U-Boats 1945-1945, Box 23,
National Archives and Record Administration, NARA,
College Park, Maryland.

```
7G - 177 - NA    WERMUTH, Otto    Oberleutnant Z, See

    1  grey leather jacket and leather trousers
    1  heavy leather belt
    1  black wool sweater
    1  white wool sweater
    1  woolen trousers
    4  pr woolen socks
    1  face towel
    1  bottle toilet water
    1  bottle "Trilysin"
    1  bottle tooth paste
    1  can XXXXXXXX can shaving cream
    1  tube "Zahnpasta"
    1  bar Life Buoy Soap
    1  box "Marfanil-Prontalbin-Puder"
    1  blue scarf
    1  light undershirt
    1  black tie
    1  pr leather gloves
    1  pr garters
    1  leather vest
    1  heavy sweater
    1  woolen watch cap
    1  light woolen underwear
    1  shirt
    1  white woolen scarf
    1  pr grey leather gloves
    3  metal buttons
    1  clothes brush
    1  German-Spanish dictionary ◄————————
```

Personal effects of Commanding Officer Oberleutnant
(Lieutenant Junior Grade) Otto Wermuth, 25 years old
U-530, Mar Del Plata, Argentina,
Arrow indicates German-Spanish dictionary

Source: Record Locator 38, OP162, Interrogations and
Documents from U-Boats 1945-1945, Box 23,
National Archives and Record Administration, NARA,
College Park, Maryland.

Mug shot of Executive Officer Oberleutnant
(Lieutenant Junior Grade) Karl Felix Schuller, 21 years old
U-530, Mar del Plata, Argentina, July 12, 1945

Source: Record Locator 38, OP162, Interrogations and
Documents from U-Boats 1945-1945, Box 23,
National Archives and Record Administration, NARA,
College Park, Maryland.

Mug shot of Commanding Officer Oberleutnant
(Lieutenant Junior Grade) Heinz Schäffer, 24 years old
U-977, Miami, Florida, September 1945

Source: Record Locator 38, OP162, Interrogations and
Documents from U-Boats 1945-1945, Box 39,
National Archives and Record Administration, NARA,
College Park, Maryland.

4

ALLEN DULLES, THE OSS, THE VATICAN, AND THE NAZI RATLINE

But the Nazis did not want to be annihilated or liquidated. They did not want to disappear. They wanted very much to go on, to go on …

—Curt Reiss, *The Nazis Go Underground* (1944)[94]

O n the morning of November 9, 1942, Henrich Himmler, the Reichsführer of the Schutzstaffel, more commonly known as the SS, held a private meeting with Martin Bormann, the head of the Parteikanzlei (the Party

---

[94] Carl Reiss, *The Nazis Go Underground* (Garden City, New York, 1944), p. 15.

Chancellery for the National Socialist German Workers' party, more commonly known as Nazis) and the personal secretary to Adolf Hitler, at the Brown House in Munich. The day before, the Allies had launched Operation Torch, an amphibious landing in French North Africa, marking the beginning of the end of the Third Reich.

Curt Riess, a former Berlin journalist who escaped Nazi Germany in the 1930s as Hitler rose to power and became an American war correspondent, noted these two men symbolized the Nazi party better than any other two found within the party ranks. "Himmler symbolized the power of the party, Bormann the rank and file," Riess wrote in his wartime book, *The Nazis Go Underground*, published in 1944. "Himmler represented the brains, Bormann the life blood of the party. Himmler knew what was necessary, Bormann knew what was possible."[95] Reiss observed that Bormann, "a stocky, bulky man, with brownish hair and without distinguishing features of any kind,"[96] never let any detail escape his attention. Himmler, as the chief of the SS and the head of the Gestapo, the Nazi state police, was one of the most feared men in Europe. "While the secret police have, in the main, been interested only in what people do or intend to do, Bormann even knows what they are likely to think under given circumstances," Reiss commented.

The reason Himmler and Bormann met on the morning of November 9, 1942, was because both knew key Nazi party members were beginning to doubt Germany would win the war. If Germany lost the war, top Nazis, including Himmler, Bormann, and possibly Hitler himself, would need a plan to escape to a safe refuge outside Germany if

---

[95] Ibid., p. 5.

[96] Ibid., p. 4.

the Nazis were to have any chance of emerging in a Fourth Reich sometime and someplace in the future.

Himmler and Bormann concluded that, in order to survive, the Nazi party had to go underground. "If Germany did not win the war, would not the Allies make good their promise and rid the world of the Nazis, or, as they were termed, the war criminals?" Reiss asked rhetorically, knowing how Himmler and Bormann would strategize their future together. "And even if they were not destroyed by the Allies, were these Nazis not threatened with annihilation at the hands of their own allies, the generals and industrialists who were eager to create alibis for themselves, even before this final defeat?"[97] What Himmler and Bormann realized was that the new front was underground.

What did it mean that the Nazi party had to go underground in order to survive? "It means that a person or a number of persons, a unit, a force, an idea, a movement that had been visible before becomes invisible. It is no longer represented to the outside world. It has become anonymous. Its existence is known only by the effects of its actions."[98]

Leaving that meeting, Himmler and Bormann began taking active steps starting in 1943 to prepare for life after Germany lost the war, even if that meant staging their own deaths, and possibly the death of Hitler, and fleeing Germany to avoid capture. But to be successful, going underground required finding and funding in advance a safe haven for post-war survival. The two best alternatives in 1942 for the post-war survival of the Nazi party rested with Argentina, and ironically, the United States of America.

---

[97]   Ibid., p. 15.

[98]   Ibid., p. 2.

Allen Dulles in Switzerland

In the 1930s, much of the financing for Hitler's rise to power came from the United States. W. Averell Harriman, US ambassador to Russia from 1943-1946, President George Herbert Walker Bush, and the Dulles brothers (John Foster Dulles who served as Secretary of State under President Eisenhower, and Allen Dulles who served as head of the CIA under both President Eisenhower and President Kennedy) have family connections that trace back to their involvement financing the Nazis. Both Prescott Bush and George Herbert Walker Bush, the grandfathers of President George Herbert Walker Bush, were partners in the Wall Street investment bank, W. A. Harriman & Company. The Dulles brothers both worked as lawyers at the prominent New York law firm Sullivan & Cromwell. In the 1930s, the Harriman family ran Union Bank in the United States in conjunction with German steel baron Fritz Thyssen, who then was widely known as "Hitler's banker." President Franklin D. Roosevelt ordered Union Bank closed only after the Japanese attacked Pearl Harbor and the United States entered World War II. Sullivan & Cromwell did the US legal work for the German chemical firm I.G. Farben, the manufacturer of Zyklon-B, the poison gas the Nazis used to kill Jews in the concentration camps.

On November 11, 1942, two days after Himmler and Bormann met privately in Munich, Allen Dulles arrived in Berne, Switzerland, just before the Germans sealed the French borders in retaliation for what Hitler perceived as half-hearted resistance by the French in North Africa to the Allied invasion then underway. The website for the National Archives and Records Administrations posted an article noting that the then 49-year-old Allen Dulles was sent to Switzerland to head up the Office of Strategic

Services, or OSS, the predecessor organization to today's CIA.[99] Originally, OSS Director William "Wild Bill" Sullivan had asked Dulles to go to London, where he could more easily coordinate between US intelligence and British intelligence. Dulles, however, prevailed with the choice of Switzerland, arguing that Berne's central position in Europe made it easier for him to gain information on the Nazis in Germany and the Fascist enemy in Italy. In Berne, Dulles set up residence at No. 23 Herrengasse and began his official appointment to serve as "Special Assistant to the American Minister." In reality, Dulles, who spent the duration of World War II in Berne, served as the United States' top spy in Europe.

On January 15, 1943, Dulles was visited in Berne by Prince Maximilian Egon zu Hohenlohe-Langenberg, whose Liechtenstein passport allowed him to travel Europe freely. The prince brought an offer from Himmler that proposed the SS would eliminate Hitler, to clear the way so Germany could join the United States and Britain to pursue the war against the Soviet Union and communism.[100] Joining in this proposal was Admiral Wilhelm Canaris, who headed Abwehr, the German intelligence organization, until February 1944. At that time, the Abwehr chief in Switzerland was Hans Bernd Gisevius, serving undercover as Vice-Counsel in the German Consulate General in Zurich. Before the outbreak of World War II, Canaris

---

[99] Dr. Greg Bradsher, "Allen Dulles and No. 23 Herrengasse, Bern, Switzerland, 194201945," National Archives website, Nov. 9, 2012, http://blogs.archives.gov/TextMessage/2012/11/09/allen-dulles-and-no-23-herrengasse-bern-switzerland-1942-1945/.

[100] Simon Dunstan and Gerrard Williams, *Grey Wolf: The Escape of Adolf Hitler – The Case Presented* (New York: Sterling Publishing, 2011), p. 17.

was active in the resistance to oppose and then overthrow Hitler, working with a group known to the SS as *Schwarze Kappelle*, or "Black Orchestra."[101] Canaris was executed for treason in 1944, after the role he played in various plots to assassinate Hitler was discovered. While Canaris never wavered in his opposition to Hitler, Himmler's instincts were much more oriented toward self-survival. Himmler may have suggested to Dulles that with the assistance of the United States, Germany would oppose the Soviet Union once Hitler was eliminated. But in other plots against Hitler proposed during the war, Himmler was happy to scheme about how he could take Hitler's position as leader of Germany if only the others would do the dirty work for him without Himmler having to be directly complicit in the plot to eliminate Hitler.

Unofficially, Dulles entertained the prince's proposal, but officially he made no commitment. What Dulles wanted to do was keep open a channel of communications with Himmler and the SS hierarchy. American intelligence officials were aware that top Nazis were preparing to go underground if Germany lost World War II, and it soon became obvious that going underground was not dependent upon a group of sensible Nazis getting rid of an irrational Führer. With or without Hitler, preserving the Nazi party remained the key goal. If Hitler survived the war, then a safe haven would be needed for him as well. The Nazi movement would not easily survive a captured Führer tried as a war criminal, even if enough money could be moved outside Germany to establish a safe haven abroad.

In one of the grandest larcenies in the history of the world, the Nazis had robbed private collections and

---

[101] Ibid.

museums in conquered territories, stolen gold from the national treasuries of defeated enemies, and robbed Jews of all valuable property down to the gold fillings in the teeth of concentration camp victims. This ill-gotten capital had been used to build Hitler's criminal war machine. With the loss of the war beginning to loom on the horizon ahead, the Nazi goal shifted from accumulating all this loot to using the loot to create and fund productive businesses overseas that were capable of generating enough revenue to sustain the escaping Nazis in predetermined havens where it would be politically safe to live, grow old, and maybe even regroup. That task fell to Bormann, the gifted organizer in the partnership with Himmler.

Bormann's empire

Beginning with the Nazi occupation of Vichy France in November 1942 and the subsequent closure of the French border, Nazi access to international art auctions held in Switzerland was cut off. Instead, Bormann established bogus art dealerships from Argentina through Latin America to Mexico in order to sell off plundered European art treasures. Bormann deposited the proceeds of these sales in two German-owned banks in Argentina: Banco Alemán Transatlántico and the Banco Germánico in Buenos Aires.[102] Baron von Schröder, an SS brigadier, was on the board of directors of some thirty different German corporations, including ITT Germany. Schröder's Bank of Hamburg was affiliated with the J. Henry Schröder & Co. of London. Also affiliated was the J. Schröder Banking Corporation of New York, for which Cromwell & Sullivan

---

[102] Ibid., p. 42.

did the legal work with Allen Dulles as a director.[103] Bormann acquired his own shipping lines, including the Spanish shipping company Compañia Naviera Levantina and the Italian Airline Linee Aeree Transcontinentali Italiane, or LATI. This gave Bormann his own independent pipeline to move people to Spain, and from Spain to Argentina, without having to use German Luftwaffe airplanes.[104]

Beginning in 1943, Bormann implemented an operation code-named *Aktion Adlerflug*, or Project Eagle Flight, with the goal of transferring German funds—whether counterfeit, stolen, or legitimate government funds—to safe havens abroad. Between 1943 and 1945, Bormann funded more than two hundred Germany companies in Argentina, with other investments in companies located in Portugal, Spain, Sweden, and Turkey. Bormann is estimated to have created some 980 front companies outside Germany, with 770 in neutral countries, including 98 in Argentina alone. Additionally, he acquired shares of foreign companies, especially those listed on North American exchanges in Canada and the United States. These investments were designed to assist prominent Nazis fleeing Germany to resume economically productive lives elsewhere. When Israeli intelligence agents captured SS Obersturmbannführer Adolf Eichmann, a major organizer of the Holocaust, in 1960, he was working under the assumed name of Riccardo Klement in the Mercedes-Benz factory established by a Bormann investment at González Catán in the suburbs of Buenos Aires.[105]

---

[103] Ibid., pp. 48-49.

[104] Ibid., p. 55.

[105] Ibid., pp. 56-58.

In the final days of World War II, Bormann was wrapped up in the dispersal of several billion dollars around the globe. "He dwelled on control of the 750 corporations [established as new German enterprises worldwide]," wrote celebrated CBS correspondent Paul Manning in his 1981 book, *Martin Bormann: Nazi in Exile*. "Bormann had utilized every known legal device to disguise their ownership and their patterns of operation: use of nominees, option agreements, poll agreements, endorsements in blank, escrow deposits, pledges, collateral loans, rights of first refusal, management contracts, service contracts, patent agreements, cartels, and withholding procedures."[106] Allen Dulles in Berne, Switzerland, had to be aware of Bormann's efforts, as German firms in the flight capital program were using six different Swiss private banks.

As Paul Manning pointed out, "all major Swiss banks were serving the Germans in the massive movement of funds," as Swiss financial agents and Swiss banks were particularly helpful to Bormann in his massive effort to diversify German capital investments outside Germany, anticipating the war would not come to a favorable end for the Nazis and Hitler's Germany.[107] Manning further commented that German economic specialists had successfully penetrated eleven nations and had the economies of each under control; Bormann cultivated a base of several hundred thousand business relationships outside Germany with companies that felt comfortable working with German economic leadership because it was always profitable. Ultimately, Bormann's web stretched across France, Belgium,

---

[106] Paul Manning, *Martin Bormann in Exile* (Secaucus, N.J.: Lyle Stuart, Inc., 1981), p. 144. Manning used the Anglicized spelling of "Mueller," instead of the German spelling, "Müller."

[107] Ibid., p. 139.

Holland, Norway, Yugoslavia, Austria, Poland, Spain, Sweden, Switzerland, Turkey, Portugal, Finland, Bulgaria, and Romania, and "reached out to such South American countries as Argentina, among others, that preferred an association with Germany to one with Britain and the United States."[108]

Even though Washington and London were aware that Bormann was shifting German capital overseas, the US Treasury was unable to successfully intervene to block Bormann's efforts. In New York, Bormann used foreign exchange funds from Swiss banks to make large demand deposits in major money center banks, including National City (now Citibank) and Chase (now J. P. Morgan Chase), and several others now defunct such as the Manufacturers and Hanover (known as Manufacturers Hanover Trust before being reorganized out of existence). In return, Manning noted, the New York money center banks provided services such as the purchases of stocks and transfer or payment of money on demand by customers of Deutsch Bank, including representatives of the Bormann business organizations and Bormann himself, who ended up with demand accounts in three different New York City banks.[109]

In developing a plan to escape to Argentina, Bormann studied up on Canaris, who as a young navy officer in World War I had been captured after the Battle of the Falkland Islands in December 1914. Canaris was held captive in Chile until he escaped in August 1915 and managed to return to Germany via Patagonia in Argentina's southern tip with the aid of some German merchants operating in Latin America. Reading a file Canaris had prepared

---

108 Ibid., p. 114.

109 Ibid., p. 139.

documenting his 1915 escape, Bormann became aware of the large German communities in sparsely populated sections of Chile and Argentina across from Antarctica. With Germany stripped of its colonies as part of the Versailles Treaty, the expatriate German communities that had thrived in South America since World War I created a perfect landing place for Nazis wishing to go underground after the defeat of Germany that Himmler and Bormann began anticipating as early as November 1942.

Then, in June 1943, a *coup d'etat* in Buenos Aries brought to power a regime sympathetic to Nazi Germany, with Argentinian military officer Colonel Juan Domingo Perón, who at the time of the coup had been a paid agent of German intelligence for two years. Seizing the opportunity, Bormann implemented another scheme code-named *Aktion Feuerland*, Project Land of Fire, in reference to the Tierra del Fuego (Spanish for "Land of Fire") at Patagonia's southernmost point.[110] "The plan's objective was to create a secret, self-contained refuge for Hitler in the heart of a sympathetic German community, at a chosen site near the town of San Carlos de Bariloche in the far west of Argentina's Rio Negro province," wrote Simon Dunstan and Gerrard Williams in their 2011 book, *Grey Wolf: The Escape of Adolf Hitler—the Case Presented.* "Here the Führer could be provided with complete protection from outsiders."

Beginning in mid-1943, Bormann's plan for Hitler's escape to Argentina was implemented by banking millionaire Ludwig Freude, Bormann's chief agent in Buenos Aires. Freude's wealth derived from the construction company he opened after he had gone to Argentina from Germany in 1913. Freude reported directly to Bormann;

---

[110] Simon Dunstan and Gerrard Williams, *Grey Wolf*, op.cit., p. 59.

by summer 1941, both Perón and his friend Eva Duarté, then a 22-year-old actress who was becoming popular on Argentinian radio, were both on Bormann's payroll.[111] Beginning in August 1942, U-boats from Germany began a run to Buenos Aries, arriving at six- to eight-week intervals in 1943 and 1944.[112] The submarines carried loot to Nazi Argentina, including gold bullion and art treasures that could not be moved via bank transfers. Estimates range as high as $50 billion in today's values for the value of the gold bullion alone that Bormann transferred to Buenos Aires via submarine, before adding in the value of the platinum, precious jewels, rare coinage, and art treasures, as well as stocks, bonds, and bearer certificates Bormann squirreled away in *Aktion Feuerland*.[113]

Dulles and the SS

At the end of World War II, Dulles, yet still operating in Berne, Switzerland, rescued Nazi intelligence director Reinhard Gehlen out of a prison camp. Under Hitler, Gehlen had been responsible for Nazi military intelligence on the Eastern Front, including the Soviet Union. Gehlen fit perfectly into the plan Dulles had masterminded to use the Nazi SS intelligence operation built by Himmler as a key element in the plan to evolve the wartime OSS into the peacetime CIA. Key to Dulles's plan was a decision by the United States to create what eventually became the postwar Allied military tribunals judging Nazi war criminals in what was known as the Nuremberg Trials. Nazi intelligence

---

[111] Ibid., p. 199.

[112] Ibid., p. 209.

[113] Ibid., p. 211.

assets like Gehlen were much too valuable to future US intelligence to be found guilty of the war crimes they had committed. Dulles's plan was to re-employ Gehlen and his network of SS intelligence agents in Eastern Europe as the backbone around which an anti-Soviet, anticommunist intelligence network could be formed, headquartered in what emerged as Western Germany and tasked with performing undercover work against communists throughout Eastern Europe.

"By the summer of 1945, Dulles had finished his negotiations with Gehlen," wrote JFK assassination researcher James DiEugenio in his 2012 book, *Destiny Betrayed: JFK, Cuba, and the Garrison Case*. DiEugenio reported that by September 1945, Gehlen and six of his aides were flown to Washington by Eisenhower's chief of staff, General Walter Bedell Smith.[114] As a result of high-level discussions in Washington, Gehlen's Nazi intelligence organization was transferred under his control to work in Eastern Europe until Germany was reorganized.

In 1949 Gehlen signed a contract to work for the CIA for five million dollars a year. In 1950 High Commissioner of Germany John McCloy appointed Gehlen as advisor to the German chancellor on intelligence. Ultimately Gehlen became intelligence chief of the Federal Republic of Germany, better known simply as West Germany. This was quite a reward for a Nazi responsible for torturing, starving, and murdering some four million Soviet prisoners of war. By rescuing Gehlen from the fate of being tried and possibly executed as a war criminal, Dulles accomplished the goal of basing US post-war intelligence efforts

---

[114]   James DiEugenio, *Destiny Betrayed: JFK, Cuba, and the Garrison Case* (New York: Skyhorse Publishing, Second Edition, 2012), pp. 4-5.

on the remnants of Himmler's Nazi SS intelligence operation. DiEugenio summarized Dulles's accomplishment as follows:

> By consummating the Gehlen deal, Allen Dulles accomplished two things. First, he signaled that the hallmark of the coming national security state would be anticommunism. Morality, honesty, common sense, these would all be sacrificed at the altar of this new god. Second, he guaranteed that the future successor to the OSS, the Central Intelligence Agency, would be compromised in a strange way: it would be viewing the new red threat not through American, but through German—indeed, Nazi— eyes, an incredible distortion, since in essence Gehlen was selling Hitler's view of the Soviet Union and communism. Not coincidentally, this was a view that dovetailed with Dulles's.[115]

Note that Allen Dulles followed General Walter Bedell Smith as CIA Director. Note also that Allen Dulles and John McCloy both ended up being appointed to the Warren Commission tasked with investigating the assassination of JFK. The Warren Commission ended up with a whitewash conclusion that Lee Harvey Oswald was the lone assassin. In what has to be one of the greatest government investigation failures of the twentieth century, the Warren Commission concluded that Lee Harvey Oswald had no connection to the FBI or the CIA, despite evidence that at the time of the assassination Oswald was being paid $200 a month to act as an informant, and the existence of a CIA file on Oswald that dated back to his defection to the Soviet Union in 1957. Prior to being appointed by

---

[115] Ibid.

President Lyndon Baines Johnson to serve on the Warren Commission, JFK, angered over Dulles's complicity in the Bay of Pigs fiasco, fired Allen Dulles as CIA director, a position he had held since being appointed by Eisenhower in 1952.

John McCloy is also infamous for a letter he wrote on November 18, 1944, when he was Assistant Secretary of War, explaining to John Pehle, then the director of the War Refugee Board, that the War Department would not authorize Pehle's request to have the Army Air Force bomb the Nazi concentration camp at Auschwitz, a move that may have saved thousands of Jews from being killed in the gas chambers.[116] The letter has been on display in the National Holocaust Museum in Washington, D.C.

Bormann escapes to Argentina

Bormann was on the long list of prominent Nazis whose bodies were never found at the end of World War II. Presuming Bormann had escaped from the Führerbunker, the International Military Tribunal at Nuremberg tried Bormann in absentia in November 1945 and, in October 1946, found him guilty and sentenced him to death, provided Bormann could ever be found. Then, in December 1972, construction workers found the remains of two corpses near the Lehrter Banhof, the site of the central train station in West Berlin, and the controversy over whether or not Bormann escaped was rekindled. At a press conference

---

[116] "John J. McCloy, Assistant Secretary of War, explains to John W. Pehle, Director, War Refugee Board, that the War Department cannot authorize the bombing of Auschwitz, Nov. 18, 1944," The American Experience, pbs.org, http://www.pbs.org/wgbh/amex/holocaust/filmmore/reference/primary/bombjohn.html.

in Frankfurt on April 11, 1973, Procurator General Horst Gauf proclaimed officially that Bormann had died on May 2, 1945, by biting down on a glass capsule containing what was described as *Blausäure*, or prussic acid. The capsule was supposedly one of 850 vials the Abwehr, the German military secret service, had ordered manufactured by the Schering pharmaceutical company for espionage operatives on perilous missions.[117]

As with Hitler, dental records were used to establish the corpse was Bormann's. The corpse was initially presumed to be Bormann's because the place of its discovery matched the account of Bormann's attempted escape from the Führerbunker published by Hugh Trevor-Roper in his 1947 book, based largely on the testimony of Hitler Youth leader Artur Axmann who claimed to have seen the corpses of Bormann and SS doctor Ludwig Stumpfegger near the railroad switching yard in Berlin, with the moon shining bright enough that their faces were clearly illuminated. According to Trevor-Roper's account, Axmann stopped for a moment when he recognized the bodies, but Russian fire kept him from examining them closely. He saw no obvious signs of wounds on either Bormann or Stumpfegger, so Axmann presumed they had been shot in the back.[118] The body of Bormann that Axmann claimed to have seen was never found subsequently, so no positive medical identification of a Bormann corpse was ever made in 1945. Axmann's unsubstantiated testimony was the only evidence that Bormann had died trying to escape the Führerbunker.

---

[117] Ladislas Farago, *Aftermath: Martin Bormann and the Fourth Reich* (New York: Simon and Schuster, 1974), pp. 26-32, at p. 27.

[118] Hugh Trevor-Roper, *The Last Days of Hitler*, op.cit., pp. 216-217.

In his 1981 book, *Martin Bormann: Nazi in Exile*, journalist Paul Manning describes three different times when he was told by three different individuals that Bormann's escape was arranged by the scheme of substituting a stand-in for his body in the freight yards of Berlin. One source was a career agent in the Secret Intelligence Service of the British Foreign Office, another served in the Federal Republic of Germany, and the third was a member of Mossad, the exterior arm of Israeli intelligence. Manning has insisted that Bormann escaped with Gestapo Chief Heinrich Müller. The first tip came over dinner in 1947, in the US press club in Frankfurt. Here is how Manning described the discussion:

> It was the day I had returned from Berlin and a personal meeting with General Lucius D. Clay, military governor of the US Zone of Occupation. General Clay had offered me the position of his civilian deputy, but I had turned it down with some reluctance, preferring to remain a European reporter for American newspapers. During the press club dinner, the British agent and I discussed the fascinating and bizarre disappearance of Reichleiter Bormann; this source said flatly that Mueller had engineered Bormann's escape, using the device of a concentration camp look-alike to throw future investigations off the scent.[119]

Then, in 1973, on a visit to Bonn, a conversation with one of General Gehlen's aides in the Federal Republic intelligence service confirmed the 1947 British tip by stating, "The skull represented as Bormann's is a fraud. Naturally the West German government wishes to bury the past and establish Bormann's death once and for all. They have been constantly

---

[119] Paul Manning, *Martin Bormann: Nazi in Exile*, op.cit., p. 180.

unsettled by continued revelations and scandals." Then, in 1978, an Israeli Mossad agent with a German specialization described to Manning the file in Tel Aviv that Israeli intelligence had never closed on Bormann. "We know he is in South America. We are not very compelled to find him because he was never personally involved in the 'final solution,'" the Israeli explained. "Bormann's business was business, and from what I know personally, he did a thorough job of shifting German assets away from the Third Reich."[120]

Manning further reported that Müller initiated his Bormann scheme in the last months of the war during a visit to the concentration camp Sachsenhausen. There Müller examined several inmates in the special elite group known as *Sonderkommando*, experts in engraving and counterfeiting who were responsible for producing counterfeit British pounds and other currencies for SS officers to use in their flight from Germany at the end of the war. Finding two inmates who resembled Bormann, Müller had them placed in special confinement where a dental room had been made for the "treatment" of the two men. A Nazi dentist worked on the mouth of each man until his teeth, real and artificial, matched Bormann's precisely.

Then, in April 1945, the unfortunate stand-ins from Sachsenhausen were killed in the Gestapo basement secret chambers with cyanide spray blown from a cigarette lighter. At Gestapo headquarters, the night of April 30, 1945, the bodies were taken by a special SS team to the freight yards near the Weidendamm Bridge and buried not too deep beneath the rubble in two different locations. Axmann discovered the first body in 1945, but the second remained buried until 1973, when a former SS man, on orders from

---

[120] Ibid.

Müller, who was then with Bormann in Argentina, leaked the information to a *Stern* magazine editor as part of a ploy to prove that Bormann had died that night in the Berlin freight yard in 1975. "The funeral and burial caper was to be a Müller trademark throughout the years of searching for Martin Bormann," Manning wrote. "The Mossad was to point out that they have been witnesses over the years to the exhumation of six skeletons, two in Berlin and four in South America, purported to be that of Martin Bormann."[121]

Respected military historian and journalist Ladislas Farago, whose acclaimed 1964 biography, *Patton: Ordeal and Triumph*,[122] formed the basis for the 1970 film, *Patton*, staring George C. Scott, wrote a controversial book in 1974—*Aftermath: Martin Bormann and the Fourth Reich*, claiming that Bormann was alive and living in Argentina.[123] Farago claimed to have been given an intelligence file in Buenos Aires from the offices of the *Secretaría de Informaciones de Estato*, or S.I.D.E., the Argentinian government's official intelligence agency. The file contained documentation that Bormann had entered Argentina in 1948, having sailed from Genoa, Italy, disguised as a Jesuit priest traveling on a second-class ticket with false documents issued by the Vatican.[124]

Farago further claimed that Bormann gained approval to enter and live in Argentina after German agent Ludwig Freude made it clear to Perón and Evita in 1947 that Freude

---

[121] Ibid., p. 183.

[122] Ladislas Farago, *Patton: Ordeal and Triumph* (New York: Ivan Obolensky, Inc., 1964).

[123] Ladislas Farago, *Aftermath: Martin Bormann and the Fourth Reich*, loc.cit.

[124] Ibid., pp. 93-95.

had arranged for the Nazi deposits made in Argentina banks to be inaccessible in Bormann's absence and without his personal participation in deciding how the funds were to be dispersed.[125] Documents made public in Argentina in 1955, after the fall of Perón, and later in 1970, showed that Perón and Evita handed over to Bormann the agreed 25 percent of the Nazi currency, gold, and platinum deposited in Argentina banks by Bormann from Germany.[126]

In 1998, the Bormann controversy surfaced once again in Germany, after German and Swiss scientists reportedly established from DNA tests that the skeleton dug up in Berlin was Bormann's. According to newspaper reports, the DNA obtained from a piece of the skull was compared to a tissue sample donated by an 83-year-old relative of Bormann's who was then living near Frankfurt.[127] But published details remain sketchy, failing to identify the scientists or the relative involved in the testing. There is no documentation that the DNA testing conducted was ever submitted to a peer-reviewed scientific or medical journal for publication.

The Vatican and the Nazi ratline

The role of the Vatican in World War II has been highly controversial. Former Romanian KGB intelligence officer Lieutenant General Ion Mihai Pacepa was the highest-ranking

---

[125] Ibid., p. 211.

[126] Simon Dunstan and Gerrard Williams, *Grey Wolf*, op.cit., p. 264.

[127] Imre Karacs, "DNA test closes book on mystery of Martin Bormann," the *Independent*, May 4, 1998, http://www.independent.co.uk/news/dna-test-closes-book-on-mystery-of-martin-bormann-1161449.html. See also: "Bormann's body 'identified,'" BBC News, May 4, 1998, http://news.bbc.co.uk/2/hi/europe/87452.stm.

Soviet bloc intelligence officer ever to defect to the West. In his 2013 book, *Disinformation*, he has argued convincingly that the construction of Pope Pius XII as "Hitler's Pope" was a KGB invention that derived from the war between communism and the Catholic Church that Pacepa described as being "almost as old as communism itself."[128] Pacepa documents the calumny traces to a Radio Moscow broadcast on June 3, 1945, that proclaimed the leader of the Catholic Church, Pope Pius XII, had been "Hitler's Pope," implying that he had been an ally of the Nazis during World War II and that he had done nothing to stop the Holocaust. Pacepa demonstrates that contrary to the Soviet propaganda, Pope Pius XII aided European Jews in World War II by diplomatic initiatives, various public pronouncements, and by promoting a network of Catholic Church sanctuary for Jews throughout Europe.

Still, there is considerable evidence that rogue elements within the Catholic Church established a monastery-based ratline to provide escaping Nazis with a way to flee Europe, many with the intended destination of Argentina. As documented by Argentina-based journalist Uki Goñi, a key player was Argentinian cardinal Antonio Caggiano, who as the bishop of the industrial city Rosario was also the leader of the Argentinian chapter of Catholic Action, a lay organization with Vatican support that had become "the rallying point for a vibrant anticommunist crusade in Argentina during the 1930s and 1940s."[129] As Goñi pointed out, Caggiano played a major role organizing mass rallies in the 1930s in support of decent housing and

[128] Ion Mihai Pacepa and Ronald J. Rychlak, *Disinformation* (Washington D.C.: WND Books, Inc., 2013), p. 59.

[129] Uki Goñi, *The Real Odessa: Smuggling the Nazis to Perón's Argentina* (London: Granta Books, 2002), p. 93.

a minimum wage that "brought together workers, nationalist activists, military officers and Catholic Action supporters in a mix that predated Perón's brand of 'Catholic populism' by only a few years."[130] Called to Rome in 1946 by Pope Pius XII to be anointed cardinal as only the second Argentinian prelate to be elevated to this high position in the Catholic Church hierarchy, Caggiano was accompanied by Augustín Barrére, the staunchly anticommunist bishop of Tucumán, Argentina. Cardinal Tisserant, the Vatican's expert on Russian affairs who dreaded the possibility of a Soviet takeover of Europe in the aftermath of World War II, assisted Caggiano and Barrére. "Through their efforts at the Vatican and their influential whispering in Perón's ear, Caggiano and Barrére paved the way for some of the worst Nazi criminals and collaborators to escape to Argentina," Goñi wrote.[131]

The way Perón's Odessa worked, a Nazi seeking to escape Europe could be issued a permit to enter Argentina from Argentina's immigration office under a false name, permitting the Nazi to obtain a Red Cross "travel document" under the same alias. Created for refugees who had lost their identification papers, Red Cross "travel documents" were the equivalent of a valid passport. With a landing permit and traveling documents in hand, the Nazi could apply at an Argentinian consulate in Europe to obtain an entry visa. Nazis on the run could leave the consulate with an Argentinian visa stamp on their Red Cross papers, with the consul issuing the immigrant an "identification certificate" that was used to obtain a *Cédula de Identidad* upon arrival in Buenos Aries. "The way was thus cleared for a successful

130   Ibid., p. 94.

131   Ibid., pp. 98-99.

escape to South America with nothing less than a change of identity thrown in," Goñi noted.[132]

Several prominent Catholic clerics played a major role in the post-war effort to help Nazis flee Europe for Argentina. Bishop Alois Hudel was a devoted National Socialist who wrote a book in 1936, *The Foundations of National Socialism*, in which he argued that Hitler was preparing the ground for the creation of a Christian Europe.[133] Hudel created a "sanctuary in Rome," through which passed thousands of former Nazi officials, some of them major war criminals or accomplices to war crimes. Another was Monsignor Krunoslav Draganovic, a Croat who was a devoted supporter of the pro-Nazi Ustasche regime led by Ante Pavelic in the ethnic mix thrown together when Yugoslavia existed as a kingdom before WWII but it was made into a Soviet republic in 1943. A figure notorious in coordinating from Argentina with the so-called "Vatican ratline" was Carlos Fuldner, born in Argentina to a German family. In 1932, Fuldner was an early recruit to the SS. A petty criminal who had to flee Germany to return to Argentina in the mid-1930, Fuldner returned to favor in Germany before the end of World War II. He was reinstated in the SS and carried both an Argentinian and a German passport as he shuttled between Berlin and Madrid on "special missions" assigned by Himmler himself. In 1948, Fuldner returned to Europe as a special agent for Perón, where he set up Nazi rescue offices in Genoa and Berne to coordinate with Draganovic and Swiss officials to smuggle Nazi war criminals to Argentina.[134]

---

[132]   Ibid., p. 124.

[133]   Ibid., p. 230.

[134]   Ibid., p. xii.

There was a natural alliance between Perón and Argentina, various elements within the Catholic Church, and the former Nazi leaders. As noted by Nazi researcher Peter Levenda in his 2012 book, *Ratline: Soviet Spies and Nazi Priests, and the Disappearance of Adolf Hitler*, all three "saw their enemy as Communism, and their natural allies in the fight against the Communists were the Nazis."[135] Among the more prominent Nazi war criminals who escaped Europe to Argentina via the Vatican ratline were the following: Josef Mengele, the infamous "Angel of Death" physician at the Auschwitz concentration camp; Klaus Barbie, the Gestapo genocidal criminal known as the "Butcher of Lyon" for his torturing of prisoners, including women and children, in France; and Adolf Eichmann, the notorious SS officer who was a major organizer of the Holocaust.

Another natural ally in this mix of the Catholic Church, former Nazis, and anticommunism was Allen Dulles, as well as the OSS operating out of Berne. James Jesus Angleton, who ultimately became the CIA chief of counter intelligence, continued working with Dulles in Switzerland even after World War II was over, coordinating US intelligence activities with the Vatican. "Angleton and Dulles laundered millions through the Vatican to defeat the Italian Communists in the elections," wrote former Justice Department Nazi hunter John Loftus and his investigative journalist co-author Mark Aarons in their 1991 book, *Unholy Trinity: The Vatican, the Nazis, and Soviet Intelligence*. "In return, the Vatican facilitated the escape of tens of thousands of Nazis to the West, where they were supposed to be trained

---

135   Peter Levenda, *Ratline: Soviet Spies and Nazi Priests, and the Disappearance of Adolf Hitler* (Lake Worth, Florida: Ibis Press, 2012), p. 69.

as 'Freedom Fighters.'"[136] By the way, Angleton, in his role as chief of CIA Counter Intelligence, serving under CIA director Allen Dulles, and as part of his responsibility for overseeing the CIA's program running military "false defectors" to the Soviet Union, was the keeper of Lee Harvey Oswald's CIA "201" personality file, which was compiled prior to the JFK assassination.[137]

Particularly controversial were the negotiations code-named "Operation Sunrise," or alternatively, "Operation Crossword," in which Allen Dulles played a direct role in negotiating the surrender of German forces in northern Italy. In his 2011 book, *Nazis on the Run: How Hitler's Henchmen Fled Justice*, historian Gerald Steinacher argues that the decision to exclude the Soviets from the Operation Sunrise negotiations with the Germans marked the beginning of the Cold War. Steinacher notes that suspicions remain that Dulles offered protection to the German Wehrmacht and SS officers in Italy during the Operation Sunrise negotiations. "Dulles had certain interests in common with the German generals and, therefore, reportedly intervened on behalf of his German partners in Sunrise," Steinacher wrote. "All SS officers who took part in the operation managed to escape serious punishment after the war. Some were later hired by US intelligence services; others were able to flee to South America or start new careers as private businessmen."[138]

---

[136]   John Loftus and Mark Aarons, *Unholy Trinity: The Vatican, the Nazis, and Soviet Intelligence* (New York: St. Martin's Press, 1991), p. xiii.

[137]   "CIA Oswald 201 File Online," Mary Ferrell Foundation, featured archive, 2008, http://www.maryferrell.org/wiki/index.php/Featured_CIA_Oswald_201_File_Online.

[138]   Gerald Steinacher, *Nazis on the Run: How Hitler's Henchmen Fled Justice* (New York: Oxford University Press, 2011), pp. 169-170.

5 | THE ESCAPE TO ARGENTINA

"From information just received from Buenos Aires, I am virtually certain Adolf Hitler and his 'wife,' Eva Braun, the latter dressed in masculine clothes, landed in Argentina and are on an immense, German-owned estate in Patagonia. The pair reportedly landed on a lonely shore from a German submarine which supposedly returned to surrender to the Allies."

—Vincent de Pascal, correspondent, *Chicago Times*, July 17, 1945[139]

---

[139] "Hitler Is Reported in Argentine Hideout: Montevideo Dispatch to Chicago Times Says Eva Braun There Too," newspaper account quotes a dispatch from Vincent de Pascal, the newspaper's Montevideo correspondent, reported in *The Lewiston Daily Sun*, July 17, 1945, http://news. google.com/newspapers?nid=1928&dat=1945 0717&id=LJ0gAAAAIBAJ&sjid=OmgFAAAAIBAJ &pg=5027,982627.

W hile in the United States, the idea that Hitler escaped the Führerbunker is considered a conspiracy theory, in Argentina few doubt that Hitler lived out the remainder of his life there in safe refuge after World War II.

In recent years, two well-known and respected journalists living in Argentina have written well-documented books explaining how Hitler arrived in Argentina at the end of World War II and lived out the remainder of his life in South America. Abel Basti, an Argentinian journalist born in the province of Buenos Aires, has written a trilogy presenting his investigations into Hitler's escape to Argentina. It began with *Bariloche Nazi: Historical Sites Related to National Socialism* (2004),[140] which was followed by *Hitler in Argentina* (2006).[141] The trilogy concluded with *Hitler's Escape: The Proof of Hitler's Escape to Argentina*, published in 2010.[142] Italian journalist Patrick Burnside's 2000 book, *The Escape of Hitler: His Invisible Life in Argentina and the Connections with Evita and Perón*,[143] has led documentary director/producer Noam Shalev and researcher Pablo Weschler to produce a new much-anticipated film dedicated to exploring the evidence in Argentina that Hitler sought refuge there at the end of World War II.[144]

[140] Abel Basti, *Bariloche Nazi: Sitios Historicos Relacionados Al Nacionalsocialismo* (Edicion del Author, 2004).

[141] Abel Basti, *Hitler en Argentina* (Edicion del Author, 2006).

[142] Abel Basti, *El Exilio De Hitler: Las pruebas de la fuga del Führer a la Argentina* (Buenos Aires, Argentina: Sudamericana, 2012).

[143] Patrick Burnside, *El Escape de Hitler: Su Vida Invisible en la Argentina, las Conexiones Con Evita y Perón* (Buenos Aires, Planeta, 2000).

[144] Michael Santo, "New 'Hitler in Argentina' documentary claims Hitler did not die in 1945," *The Examiner*, Dec. 31, 2012,

The problem for most United States readers is that books published in Argentina on Hitler's escape generally have not been translated into English, and the Spanish editions are hard to get and relatively expensive even when purchased from Internet book-buying powerhouse distributors that carry foreign-language titles. Reading these books in Spanish makes it clear that Basti and Burnside have conducted extensive interviews with those few World War II eyewitnesses to Hitler's arrival yet alive in Argentina. Moreover, each journalist has spent years conducting primary research in Argentina, involving the seeking-out of contemporary World War II newspaper accounts published in Argentina and examining in the government archives in Buenos Aires the limited documentary evidence that has been made public on a topic that has remained politically sensitive despite the passage of more than six decades since the end of World War II. Perhaps because so many of the primary sources remain in Argentina in Spanish, English-speaking readers in the United States have had little access to the folklore widely accepted as common knowledge in Argentina that Hitler escaped from Germany and arrived by submarine in 1945, landing in Mar del Plata on the Atlantic coast 400 kilometers (249 miles) south of Buenos Aires.

As we saw in Chapter Three, US military intelligence in Germany had information as early as September 1945 that Hitler had escaped to Argentina with the help of Walter and Ida Bonfert Eichhorn, German expatriates who had financially supported him early on, around the time of the Munich Beer Hall Putsch in 1923. We also saw that J. Edgar Hoover wrote to the US

Embassy in Buenos Aires in November 1945, warning US diplomats in Argentina that the FBI had information that Mrs. Eichhorn, the proprietor of a spa in La Falda, Argentina, had made repeated offers to create a safe haven for Hitler in Argentina. Interestingly, this information which was available to US authorities within months of Hitler's disappearance turns out to be the current focus of the books published since 2000 by Abel Basti and Patrick Burnside. From Mar del Plata, the trail, as we shall see, connects Mr. and Mrs. Eichhorn and "The Eden," the elaborate hotel and resort complex built in the 1890s that was acquired by Walter Eichhorn and his brother Bruno in 1912, in the town of La Falda in the province of Córdoba, approximately 800 kilometers (498 miles) northwest of Buenos Aires.[145] From there, the trail for Hitler in Argentina traces to San Carlos de Bariloche, a small town in the province of Rio Negro at the southernmost tip of Argentina. In many ways, San Carlos de Bariloche resembles the German Alps, situated as it is in the foothills of the Andes and on the southern shores of Nahuel Hapi Lake. The region is noted for the large number of German expatriates who have settled here since the beginning of the twentieth century.

The flight of the wolf

Even as these Argentinian researchers turned their attention to how exactly Hitler escaped from Berlin, their conclusions remain shrouded in uncertainty. Still, after sorting through the available evidence, two different stories have emerged as the leading contenders for the truth. Hitler,

---

[145] Ronald C. Newton, *The "Nazi Menace" in Argentina, 1931-1947* (Palo Alto, California: Stanford University Press, 1992), p. 77.

whose private nickname for himself was "The Wolf," did not decide to commit suicide rather than risk capture. Instead, the Führer decided to flee, heeding the advice of his closest advisors.

The two co-conspirators urging Hitler to escape appear to have been Martin Bormann, Hitler's secretary, and Henrich Müller, the head of the Gestapo. "Bormann's power over Hitler began with the murder of Hitler's niece, Angelica ('Geli') Raubal, who catered to Hitler's perverted sexual needs," wrote journalist William Stevenson in his 1973 book, *The Bormann Brotherhood*.[146] Although the incident remains shrouded in secrecy even today, the likelihood is that Hitler shot and killed her in a fit of jealous rage on September 18, 1931 in his apartment, into which Geli had moved at Hitler's insistence. She was 23 years old at the time. Among the investigators called to the spot was Henrich Müller, then a local police detective. "Müller found the girl lying dead beside what turned out to be Hitler's revolver," Stevenson continued. "Her naked body was bruised and her nose was broken."[147] Bormann arrived at an understanding with Müller that involved shipping Geli's body back to Vienna in a sealed lead coffin. Her death was ruled a suicide and the investigation was quietly closed. Müller rose within Nazi ranks to become the head of the Gestapo. Müller, like Bormann, is one of the top Nazis whose body was never found when Berlin fell to the Soviets on May 2, 1945. In September 1963, Müller's "grave" at the Lilienthalstrasse Cemetery in West Berlin was exhumed

---

[146] William Stevenson, *A New Investigation of the Escape and Survival of Nazi War Criminals* (New York: Harcourt Brace Jovanovich, Inc., 1973), p. 30.

[147] Ibid.

and the grave was found to contain the remains of three different people, none of whom were Müller.[148]

On the night of April 22, 1945, two days after his birthday, Hitler was walking his favorite dog Blondi when he met Müller in the garden of the Chancellery outside the Führerbunker. Also present in the garden at that time were Heinz Linge, Hitler's valet, and SS General Hans Rattenhuber, the head of Hitler's personal bodyguard. This, according to several different accounts, is the night Hitler left Berlin. Supposedly, when Hitler left the garden that night, Rattenhuber commented, "The Chief is gone, but now we have a new Chief," referring to Hitler's double assuming the role of Hitler in the Führerbunker.

Eyewitnesses in the Führerbunker noted a distinct difference between the Hitler they observed before and after April 22, 1945. Before this date, Hitler was alert, afterwards he was dull and drowsy; before Hitler could climb up the forty-eight steps to the bunker exit, afterwards he could barely climb two steps; before he slept late and preferred late night conferences, afterwards he had breakfast at 8:30 a.m. and only held short afternoon conferences; before he had lunch with Eva Braun, afterwards he avoided all social contact with her.[149]

In an interview on Feb. 7, 1948, Gertraud Junge, the secretary who claimed to have typed Hitler's last will and

---

[148]   Timothy Naftali, Norman J. W. Goda, Richard Breitman, and Robert Wolfe, "Analysis of the Name File of Heinrich Mueller," National Archives, Interagency Working Group, Record Group 263, Records of the Central Intelligence Agency, Records of the Directorate of Operations, http://www.archives.gov/iwg/declassified-records/rg-263-cia-records/rg-263-mueller.html.

[149]   H. D. Baumann, *Hitler's Fate: The Final Story* (Twickenham, United Kingdom: Athena Press, 2008), p. 58.

testament as dictated to her by Hitler, commented in passing on a very different Hitler and Eva Braun than was expected. "His eyes were no longer in this world; they did not penetrate one any more," she noted. "For instance, it has been like that that during those days people smoked in his presence. Even Eva Braun smoked."[150] Interviewing her, Musmanno was surprised. He noted that Eva Braun had never smoked before, and Junge agreed. Hitler, who never smoked, was typically intolerant of anyone who dared smoke around him. That Hitler had a double in the Führerbunker is clear from the lookalike corpse with a bullet hole in its forehead that the Soviets, assuming the body was Hitler's, displayed in a Soviet propaganda film made after the fall of Berlin. If Hitler's double was substituted for him the night of April 22, 1945, this would lend weight to the supposition that Hitler's last will and testament, as well as his marriage to Eva Braun, were events staged most likely by Goebbels with the intent of lending credence to the suicide story by showing that Hitler in his last hours was intent on wrapping up the loose strings of his messy personal life.

Some accounts have Hitler fleeing Berlin on board a Focke-Achgelis Fa-223 twin-rotor helicopter that the Nazis had developed. The helicopter supposedly flew to Hörsching airfield outside Linz, Austria. From there, Hitler flew to Barcelona, Spain, on April 26, 1945, in a Junkers 290 A6 airplane piloted by the highly decorated German Luftwaffe bomber pilot, Werner Baumbach.

---

[150] Interview with Gertraud Junge, Munich, Feb. 7, 1948, in the Michael Musmanno Collection, Gumberg Library Digital Collections, Duquesne University, p. 44, http://digital.library.duq.edu/cdm-musmanno/item_viewer.php?CISOROOT=/musmanno-interviews&CISOPTR=25&CISOBOX=1&REC=1.

Barcelona was an ideal location for escape both because of the sympathy Spain's dictator Francisco Franco had for Hitler (going back to Hitler's support of Franco during the Spanish Civil War) and because the seaport city made an escape by U-boat possible. In his 2012 book, *El Exilio De Hitler*, Basti notes that Baumbach mentions in his autobiographical book, *Broken Swastika*, that he was in Berlin on April 21, 1945, to meet with Albert Speer. Here, Baumbach inserts a strange sentence that Basti considered completely out of context. Baumbach wrote: "We had fixed up long-range aircraft and flying-boats so that we could get anywhere on earth."[151] Basti observes that Baumbach does not explain why he was in Berlin on April 21, 1945, nor does he explain what he was doing from April 21 to April 28, 1945.[152]

Basti also claims to have in his archives a Nazi document that lists the official passenger manifest from Hörsching airfield to Barcelona at 20:00 hours military time on April 26, 1945. The passenger manifest lists, in addition to Hitler and Eva Braun, that the additional passengers included Bormann and Müller, as well as SS officer Hermann Fegelein, the brother-in-law of Eva Braun.[153] The names of Goebbels and his wife and children were originally included on the list, but appear to have been crossed out, indicating that the Goebbels family did not make the flight. This is consistent with the evidence that the Goebbels family committed suicide, with their corpses positively identified in the Führerbunker. After World

---

151   Werner Baumbach, *Broken Swastika: The Defeat of the Luftwaffe* (New York: Dorset Press, 1960), p. 193.

152   Abel Basti, *El Exilio De Hitler*, op.cit., p. 231.

153   Ibid., pp. 236-239.

War II, Basti noted, Baumbach traveled to live in Argentina, where in 1948 he was named "technical consultant" to the Argentinian air force. In 1953, he was killed in an air accident when he was testing the launch from a British Avro Lancaster B-036 bomber of a missile developed in Argentina with the collaboration of the Nazis.[154]

U-530 surfaces at Mar del Plata

At dawn on July 10, 1945, the 76.8-meter (252-foot) long Type IXC/40 German submarine U-530 surfaced unexpectedly outside the harbor at Mar del Plata. Commanding Officer Oberleutnant (Lieutenant Junior Grade) Otto Wermuth, 25 years old, and Executive Officer Oberleutnant (Lieutenant Junior Grade) Karl Felix Schuller, 21 years old, were the two most senior officers aboard. At 6:30 a.m., Wermuth ordered the navigation lights lit, and the submarine began entering the harbor. In response to signals from shore, he flashed with his blinker the letters "A-L-E-M-A-N-A S-U-B-M-A-R-I-N-O ("German submarine). He proceeded cautiously, flying the Nazi flag.

According to US Navy intelligence reports, the U-530 made a dawn entry into the Mar del Plata harbor, skillfully negotiating a sand band that partially obstructs the channel and making its entrance despite the lights of the town that make lights at the end of the breakwater marking the entrance to the harbor exceedingly difficult to distinguish. On July 23, 1945, *Time magazine* described the arrival of the U-530 as follows:

> Off the submarine base at swank Mar del Plata, fishermen trolled through the wintry, misty Argentinian dawn. Out of the grey murk loomed the bulk of a big

---

[154]   Ibid., p. 240.

submarine. Its engines silent, it rolled gently with the waves. The fishermen noted the craft's unfamiliar lines, went right on fishing. Just before daylight, the submarine got under way, slid silently through the naval base's narrow entrance. The sub swished past a sentry, standing with his back to the sea, and blinked a surrender signal to the control tower. The German submarine, U-530, commanded by Lieut. Otto Wermuth, 25, had arrived.[155]

Argentinian naval officers ordered the U-530 to secure a buoy in the outer harbor. The officers and crew were taken off and lodged in the Naval Base under guard. Once the crew was on shore, the Argentinian navy began taking an inventory of all gear on board the submarine. Preparations were made to start interrogating the prisoners. Argentinian naval officers Captain José Dellepiane and Commander Patricio J. Conway, both considered by US naval intelligence to be favorable to the US cause, were assigned to lead the interrogations, and the US and British Embassies were invited to send observers, but the request was made that no publicity be given to this offer for "political" reasons.[156]

The extremely corroded condition of the ship's hull indicated that the U-530 had been at sea for a long time, but US navy intelligence could not determine by inspection the exact duration of its journey. A US navy intelligence report dated July 13, 1945, commented, "There appears to be no reason why the sub could not have

---

[155] *Time Magazine*, "Argentina: U-530," Vol. XLVI, No. 4, July 23, 1945.

[156] Naval Attaché, Buenos Aires, Argentina, US Navy Intelligence Report, "Subject: German Submarine Surrenders to Argentine Navy," July 13, 1945. Source: Record Locator 38, OP162, Interrogations and Documents from U-Boats 1945-1945, Box 23, National Archives and Record Administration, NARA, College Park, Maryland. Appears to be a mimeograph copy.

returned to a European port before coming here and have brought passengers." The report also indicated skepticism about Wermuth's claim that he came to Argentina because he considered it a safe haven, and he did not know that Argentina had declared war on Germany. "Since he stated his radio was in good condition, it can be assumed he did know," the US navy intelligence report continued, indicating suspicion that the commanding officer was lying. "Since this is at variance with his statement as to the condition of his radio, it is believed that he had other reasons for coming to Argentina." The report noted that rumors were being investigated about fisherman off the coast of Argentina seeing a strange submarine on July 9, 1945, the day before the U-530 surfaced at Mar del Plata. Other rumors suggested a submarine off the coast was seen a week before the U-530 surrendered. "Had it been the intention to land people, this would be a logical procedure—land the people and then stand off for some time in order to give those people an opportunity to hide themselves before the possibility of their landing from a submarine could be noted."[157]

In his initial discussions with Argentinian navy officials, Wermuth indicated that there were fifty-four sailors on board the U-530: the commanding officer, plus two deck officers, two engineer officers, and forty-nine men. Wermuth explained that the U-530 left Kiel, Germany, north of Hamburg, on February 19, 1945, after overhauling there. The submarine proceeded to Kristiansand, Norway, and left there in March, assigned to patrol the North Sea and North Atlantic. Wermuth explained that the U-530 spent some time off the port of New York. He said that the U-530 departed with full tanks, holding

---

[157]   Ibid.

245 tons of diesel oil, with six tons left on arrival. The vessel was capable of making eighteen knots on the surface and five knots submerged with the snorkel up. Wermuth noted that he had not used the snorkel "for a long time."[158] The oldest member of the crew was a 45-year-old warrant officer, and one of the engineers was 32 years old—but the rest of the crew averaged about 22 years old, with the youngest being 19. The crew was examined by an Argentinian medical officer and found to be in good health, although all were pale, apparently due to having been submerged during daylight hours, which the crew claimed had been the case.[159]

Was Hitler on the U-530?

On July 11, 1945, the day after the U-530 surfaced in Mar del Plata harbor, the Argentinian Ministry of Marine issued a communiqué stating that the interrogation of the crew and inspection of the submarine proved that the U-530 did not carry any Germany politicians or military officials, no persons were landed on the Argentinian coast prior to survival, and all personnel aboard were bona fide crew members. From the Mar del Plata naval station, the officers and crew were taken under guard to Martín García, a small detention island in the Río de la Plata, after the Argentinian Cabinet decided on July 17, 1945, that the submarine and crew would be placed at the disposal of US and British authorities, with the findings of Argentinian naval authorities also turned over. US naval intelligence was suspicious that the Argentinian government authorities, yet

---

[158]   Ibid.

[159]   Ibid.

sympathetic to Nazi Germany, had forced what amounted to whitewash conclusions.

In a US naval intelligence report written on July 18, 1945, the Naval Attaché in Buenos Aires noted that Argentinian newspapers had reported the following: "None of the crew has identification papers, the combat-log is missing, all armament was destroyed or rendered useless, the bow gun and two anti-aircraft guns are missing, and the only ammunition left aboard is in such condition as to be useless." Clearly the crew had something to hide, and the submarine was not ready for combat before it surrendered to Argentinian naval authorities. The US naval intelligence report further commented, "There was plenty of food aboard but very little fuel. The crew was in good condition and very little information of value could be gotten from any of them. The ship's log and instruments were intact and the submarine was fitted with a particularly powerful radio which was in operating condition. The crew of fifty-four men was sixteen over the normal crew of thirty-eight men for a submarine of that class."

The report went on to describe a C-4 naval intelligence report that tracked various unnamed Argentinian newsmen who were following stories that Hitler and Eva Braun had been landed in the south of Argentina. The critical paragraph containing that information is reproduced here in full:

> A submarine was sighted by an Argentinian Navy transport about the middle of June and was subsequently hunted by Argentinian warships. Two men landed near San Julián (Territory of Santa Cruz) about July 1, 1945, coming in a rubber boat and

being met by a sailing boat. The submarine refueled from drums hidden under water along the coast at a place marked with three large stones near a tamarisk grove. Another submarine is on the way to Argentina to surrender. The Assistant Chief of the Department of Investigations informed the Federal Police that a submarine was going to surrender some time before the actual surrender took place. Eva BRAUN and Adolf HITLER were landed in the south of Argentina.[160]

Interestingly, even though this paragraph was written to report on what Argentinian news reporters were saying, the last sentence regarding Adolf Hitler and Eva Braun was written as if the information conveyed were established fact. The report noted that in police circles, it was being said that U-530 put in at Comodoro Rivadavia before surrendering at Mar del Plata. Further more, a resident of Coronel Dorrego, Province of Buenos Aires, reported that on or about June 22, 1945, some people landed on the coast from a rubber boat.

In addition, on the evening of July 9, the day before the U-530 surrendered, a celebration was held in the private dining room of what US Navy intelligence characterized as the "Nazi Jousten Hotel" to laud the arrival of some important Nazis in Argentina. The report continued to note that celebrations were also held in other Nazi meeting places for the same reason. "On July 17, the same source reported that

---

[160] Naval Attaché, Buenos Aires, Argentina, US Navy Intelligence Report, "Subject: Argentina Navy, Movements of Enemy Vessels," July 18, 1945. Source: Record Locator 38, OP162, Interrogations and Documents from U-Boats 1945-1945, Box 23, National Archives and Record Administration, NARA, College Park, Maryland. Appears to be a mimeograph copy.
Capitalization and parenthesis in original.

HITLER and five other men had landed (time and place unknown) in a restricted military district far in the south of Argentina," the US Navy intelligence report stressed. "They are said to have come in from the sea in two power boats, flying the Argentinian official flag."[161]

U-530's clandestine mission

A careful reading of the US naval intelligence reports on the U-530 investigation makes it clear that the navy believed the officers and crew of the U-530 were lying, with many clues suggesting that the U-530 was on a clandestine mission, most likely involving the ferrying of high-profile Nazis to safety in Argentina.

A US naval intelligence report filed from Buenos Aires dated July 25, 1945, indicated that the U-530 was found to be short one large rubber life raft. The report noted that life rafts were carried in waterproof containers on deck and were equipped with a sack of yellowish chemical that, when loosened in seawater, dyed it a very bright green. The life rafts were orange colored, and the dye was presumed to make the life rafts more visible from the air. It was noted that the container just forward of the conning tower, which was closed when the U-530 arrived at Mar del Plata, did not contain a life boat, but was filled with a bright green liquid, presumably dyed seawater. "Attention is called to the fact that if one boat were used for some purpose clandestinely, it might be assumed that the dye would be left in the container, and seawater could easily have splashed into the container," the report commented. To document and reference the specifics of the mission raft, US naval intelligence most likely suspected, but could

---

[161] Ibid. Capitals and parenthesis in original.

not prove that the missing life raft had been used to ferry important passengers from the U-530 to friendly forces on shore, anticipating important Nazi guests who had escaped from Germany.[162]

The US navy intelligence reports also state suspicions that Wermuth, who was only 25 years old, may not have actually been the commanding officer of the U-530—but that the real commanding officer may have been landed somewhere else. Another stated suspicion is that the additional fourteen crew members beyond the thirty-eight needed to run the ship may have been picked up from another U-Boat that was scuttled along the Argentinian shore after dropping off the Nazi officials transported from Germany. Was the U-530 stripped of armaments and torpedoes to allow the submarine to take on the extra weight from a crew of VIP Nazis picked up in Europe and/or a U-boat crew picked up in Argentina upon completion of their transport of VIP Nazis to the Atlantic coast? Argentinian researchers Juan Salinas and Carlos De Nápoli discuss in their 2002 book, *Ultramar Sur* (*Overseas South*), available only in a Spanish edition, that at least five German U-boats reached Argentina in the months at the end of World War II, carrying no fewer than fifty high-ranking Third Reich officials on board. The authors believe that their crews scuttled several of these U-boats after the

---

[162] Naval Attaché, Buenos Aires, Argentina, US Naval Intelligence, "Report on the Interrogation of Prisoners from U-530 Surrendered at Mar del Plata, 10 July 1945, dated July 24, 1945. Source: Record Locator 38, OP162, Interrogations and Documents from U-Boats 1945-1945, Box 23, National Archives and Record Administration, NARA, College Park, Maryland. Appears to be a black-ink typed copy.

passengers were dropped off along Argentina's southern Atlantic shore.[163]

The officers and crew of the U-530 were noted to be evasive in answering questions, both when interrogated by Argentinian naval officials in Mar del Plata and when questioned by US naval officials both in Argentina and later in Washington. The US intelligence reports on the interrogation found gaps and inconsistencies in the accounts, concluding that there was nothing to preclude the U-530 from having stopped in Europe to pick up passengers before heading across the Atlantic toward Argentina. US interrogators noted that Wermuth "talked very freely in general, but consistently refused to give information about specific routes and areas." Interrogators noted that Karl Schuller, the second-in-command, was "very non-cooperative," refusing to answer many questions. In general, all fifty-four sailors stuck to the same cover story, almost as if it had been rehearsed: that the ship had been overhauled in Kiel, Germany, and then sailed in March 1945 from Kristiansand, Norway, to patrol the Atlantic. Wermuth continued to insist that he received a message on May 8 that the war in Europe had stopped. He said that although at the time they knew Argentina had broken diplomatic relations with Germany, he did not know Argentina had declared war on Germany. He insisted that he decided to come to Argentina for the internment because it was far from the fighting zone in Europe and because he thought they would get better treatment there. Since all log books and navigation records were destroyed before the U-530

[163] Juan Salinas and Carlos De Nápoli, *Ultramar Sur: La última operación secreta del Tercer Reich* (Buenos Aires, Argentina: Grupo Editorial Norma, 2002).

reached Mar del Plata, there was no way to determine precisely where the ship had been and when.

Again, various clues suggest Wermuth was lying. Among the inventory of the crew's personal effects that Argentinian naval authorities had prepared, Wermuth was found to have had on board with him a German-Spanish dictionary, an item several other sailors had listed in their personal inventories as well. There hardly seems any reason for the crew of the U-530 to have gone to sea with German-Spanish dictionaries if their sole purpose was to patrol the Atlantic in combat missions. If Wermuth had the German-Spanish dictionary from the beginning of the voyage, that suggests his mission departing from somewhere in Europe may have been to sail to Argentina, not to engage in combat in the Atlantic. The alternative would be to assume that Wermuth and other sailors found to have Spanish dictionaries picked them up in one of the stops the U-530 may have made along the Argentinian coast dropping off Nazi passengers. Other sailors were found to have Argentinian cigarettes, Argentinian chocolate, and Argentinian pesos amongst their possessions. Again, Argentinian cigarettes hardly seem a normal item issued by the German navy, but picking up Argentinian cigarettes from compatriots on shore receiving their Nazi guests could easily have been part of a welcoming ceremony.

The U-977 surfaces at Mar del Plata

Then, on August 17, 1945, a second Nazi U-boat, the U-977, came to the surface outside Mar del Plata harbor and surrendered, five weeks after the U-530 did the same. This U-boat was a 220-foot Type VIIC/41 with a standard crew of fifty-two and was considered to be the workhorse of the German U-boat force. Unlike the U-530, the U-977 arrived in Argentina fully armed with a full complement of torpedoes on board. The commanding officer, Oberleutnant (Lieutenant Junior Grade) Heinz Schäffer was 24 years old at the time the U-977 was surrendered in Argentina. The U-977 left Kristiansand, Norway, on May 2, 1945, the day after Germany announced Hitler's death. This was the U-977's first and only war patrol. The objective was to move into the port of Southampton, in Great Britain, to attack British shipping. The U-977 had reached the waters of Scotland when on May 5, 1945, German President Karl Dönitz ordered all German submarines to return to their home ports. According to the engineering officer, U-977 left Kristiansand with only eighty-five metric tons of fuel and arrived at Mar del Plata with approximately five tons. U-977, as a Type VIC/41 U-boat, was capable of doing seventeen knots on the surface and 7.6 knots submerged. On this last patrol, the U-977 spent 107 days at sea, for an elapsed cruise of 7,644 nautical miles.

On May 8, 1945, when the German surrender became official and after extensive discussions on board, several of the crew wished to disembark and return home. On May 10, 1945, between 0230 and 0330 hours military time, three enlisted men and thirteen petty officers took three of the large rubber boats, one of which was damaged and abandoned, and sixteen of the one-man rubber boats, and put ashore at the island of Holsenöy, near Bergen, Norway. After the departure of these sixteen members of the crew, the U-977 continued with the remaining thirty-two officers and men.[164] Those who remained with the submarine

---

[164]   Office of Naval Intelligence, "Report on the Interrogation of Prisoners from U-977 Surrendered at Mar Del Plata, 17 August 1945," File Op-16-2, Sept. 19, 1945, http://www.uboatarchive.net/U-977INT.htm.

hoped to avoid being turned over to the Russians. They planned instead to surrender to the Argentinians, with the hope of being allowed to settle in South America. In a book written by Schäffer in 1952, the cruise of the U-977 to Argentina was distinguished by Schäffer's claim to have sailed an extraordinary sixty-six days continuously submerged, using the snorkel to recharge the electric batteries.[165] This is a claim Schäffer evidently neglected to make to interrogators immediately after his surrender. The US Navy report on U-977 crew interrogations, compiled a month after the submarine's capture, mentions nothing about a sixty-six-day voyage submerged. Specifically, the US Navy report notes that the U-977 made for an Iceland Passage after dropping off the sixteen crewmates in Norway, diving once on sighting an airplane and once on sighting a ship. That the U-977 was forced to dive implies that the submarine was on the surface at the time.[166] The US Navy report also notes that the U-977 anchored for four hours on July 14, 1945, on the southwest side of Branco in Cape Verde to permit the crew to take a swim.

Schäffer has always insisted that the U-977 played no part in Hitler's or any other Nazi official's escape from Europe to Argentina. Yet in his 1952 book, he describes being brought before an Anglo-American Commission composed of high-ranking officers dispatched to Argentina to investigate the U-977. "These gentlemen were very

---

[165] Heinz Schaefer, *U-Boat 977* (New York: W. W. Norton & Co. Inc., 1952); republished as Heinz Schaeffer, *U-Boat 977: The U-Boat that Escaped to Argentina* (Bristol, United Kingdom: Cerberus Publishing Ltd., 2003), Chapter 13, "Sixty-Six Days Under Water," pp. 131-137.

[166] Office of Naval Intelligence, "Report on the Interrogation of Prisoners from U-977 Surrendered at Mar Del Plata, 17 August 1945," loc.cit.

obstinate indeed," Schäffer wrote. "'You have stowed Hitler away,'" they told me. "'Come on, where is he?'" Schäffer wrote that every story written about him focused not on "this first long underwater journey under such conditions," but upon suspicions that he had been involved in Hitler's escape. He described that, when he was handed over to the United States and placed in a camp for VIP POWs in Washington, D.C., the questioning continued. "For weeks on end, day after day, the Americans repeated the charge: 'You stowed Hitler away.' For weeks on end I tried to make them see how nonsensical the whole thing was—actually I could no more prove that I hadn't than they could show that I had, which simply brought us to a deadlock."[167] Finally, the Americans put Schäffer in a room together with Otto Wermuth, the commanding officer of the U-530. "They were hoping that in the first flush of our joyful reunion we would so far forget ourselves as to discuss, in front of all their Dictaphones, the whole inside story of the ghost convoy," Schäffer wrote. "They must have been very annoyed when nothing emerged from our talk save the true facts about the completely independent voyages of both our submarines."[168]

Yet claims persist that U-977 was involved in shielding other U-Boats unloading Nazi VIPs along the Atlantic coast of Argentina. When the U-977 surrendered at Mar del Plata, the submarine was observed to have suffered unexplained depth charge damage and to have been repainted. The U-977 may well have been the submarine depth-charged by the Argentinian torpedo boat "Mendoza" near San Antonio del Oeste on July 18, 1945. Other suspicions

---

[167] Heinz Schaeffer, *U-Boat 977: The U-Boat that Escaped to Argentina*, 2003 edition, pp. 154-155.

[168] Ibid., p. 155.

are that the real reason Schäffer disembarked crew in Norway was not that the crew members leaving the submarine were married and wanted to go home at the end of the war, but because the U-977 needed to make room for a previously unscheduled stop to pick up Nazi VIP passengers needing to escape Europe. Perhaps a rendezvous to pick up Nazi elite was the point of the stop on the Cape Verde Islands rather than a need to provide submariners used to underwater duty with a chance to get some fresh air and take a swim. Schäffer also never fully explained why it took from July 23 to August 17, 1945, some forty-five days, to go from the equator to Mar del Plata, a distance of less than 3,300 miles, except to establish the presumption that his record underwater stint slowed the submarine down to a crawl. Experts calculating from Schäffer's testimony to the US Navy indicate that U-977 was averaging a speed of ten nautical miles per hour, a speed which should have permitted the U-boat to travel some 276 miles per day while cruising the South Atlantic, which would have placed the submarine at the point of surrender on August 5, 1945. Was the extra time used to discharge Nazi passengers, or to guard other U-boats engaged in that activity? Clearly the intensity of the US interrogation as reported by Schäffer suggests his innocent story was not so readily believed.[169]

A refuge in Bariloche

When Hitler arrived in Argentina, he found an enthusiastic German community ready to welcome his presence. In 2010, Argentinians of German descent account for more than three million in a population that approaches forty-two million, with many of these families having emigrated

---

[169] H. D. Baumann, *Hitler's Escape*, op.cit., p. 154.

from Germany in the decades preceding World War I. In the 1930s, as Hitler came to power, many German-Argentinians were fierce Nazi sympathizers dedicated to the principles of national socialism. In the spring of 2008, some 20,000 Nazi supporters celebrated a "Day of Unity" rally held at the Luna Park stadium in Buenos Aires to celebrate the Anschluss, the annexation of Austria into the Third Reich, with German Nazi flags flying alongside the Argentinian flag.[170]

As suggested earlier in this chapter, Hitler found an immediate refuge at the Eden Hotel, owned by Walter and Ida Bonfert Eichhorn, in La Falda in the province of Córdoba. Now in disrepair, the Eden Hotel was a focal point for the German community in Argentina in the period leading up to and during World War II. During this period, the Eden Hotel had international prestige, hosting heads of state from Europe and distinguished guests, including physicist Albert Einstein. Every time the Nazis won a major victory on the battlefield, the Eden Hotel was the site of celebrations and parties. Abel Basti, in his book *Hitler en Argentina*, documents that Hitler and the Eichhorns freely exchanged letters and were on cordial terms. The Eichhorns, visiting Germany once a year before the war, supported Hitler's political campaigns financially as he rose to power. As an expression of gratitude, Hitler sent Ida Eichhorn a personal gift of the first Mercedes-Benz automobile to arrive in South America.[171]

In 1943, architect Alejandro Bustillo (at the request of German supporters of Hitler then living in Argentina)

---

[170] Simon Dunstan and Gerrard Williams, *Grey Wolf*, op.cit., p. 197.

[171] Abel Basti, *El Exilio De Hitler*, loc.cit. See also: "Revealed: Hitler in Argentina," YouTube, posted Dec. 24, 2012, http://www.youtube.com/watch?feature=player_embedded&v=Gw1hgOlHTD4.

designed and constructed an elaborate resort residence for Hitler and Eva Braun—*Residencia Inalco*, located in a remote area between San Carlos de Bariloce and Villa La Angostura, bordering the Nahuel Haupi Lake outside the city of Bariloche, in the province of Río Negro, Argentina. Hitler's Inalco *estancia*, a home of 6,000 square feet built on 1,050 acres of land on the banks of the lake, is protected on all sides by dense forests. In its heyday, the ten-bedroom mansion had a large expanse of private beach and a dock suitable for mooring seaplanes.[172] The Hitler mansion was built to look and feel Bavarian, located in "an area of outstanding natural beauty, with snowcapped mountains and several lakes set amid mile after mile of untouched forest."[173] Here in southern Argentina, in the region of the Andes adjoining Chile, the surroundings and residence were selected and designed to echo the distinct feel of Hitler's Obersalzberg retreat above the town of Berchtesgaden in the Bavarian Alps. Hitler moved into the residence in June 1947.

---

[172] "Residencia Inalco: la casa de Hitler en Argentina," HistoriasLadoB. blogspot.com, March 5, 2012, http://historiasladob.blogspot. com/2012/03/residencia-inalco-la-casa-de-hitler-en.html.

[173] Simon Dunstan and Gerrard Williams, *Grey Wolf*, op.cit., p. 252.

Conclusion

WHO HELPED HITLER ESCAPE?

Today I know that the great Bormann mystery was never really a mystery at all. His survival was known to the governments of countries in whose territories he lived with impunity since 1948.

—Ladislas Farago, *Aftermath: Martin Bormann and the Fourth Reich* (1974)[174]

That Hitler escaped Berlin was never a mystery to Juan Perón, as Hitler even today is widely believed by Argentinians to have lived out his life in Argentina. Still, that Hitler escaped Berlin alive and lived out the remainder of his life in a mountain lake retreat in Argentina is an outrage when we consider that countless

---

[174] Ladislas Farago, *Aftermath: Martin Bormann and the Fourth Reich*, op.cit., p.36.

millions—certainly more than sixty million—died in World War II, with more than six million Jews murdered in the Holocaust.

A key theme of this book is that the cover story of Hitler's dual suicide with his new bride Eva Braun has become the official politically correct version of Hitler's demise because that version was and is more palatable to establishment leaders in the United States and Europe. At the end of the war, Eisenhower knew that Hitler had escaped, and he had the courage to say so, at least up until the time when he was preparing to run for president.

In reality, very few Nazis were ever brought to justice. The Nuremberg Trials, in which twenty-three of the most important Nazi political and economic figures then in captivity were tried, was the most important war crimes tribunal held by the Allies in Europe at the end of World War II. While sixteen Nazis were hanged to death at the conclusion of the Nuremberg Trials, tens of thousands of Nazis escaped Europe, largely heading to Argentina and other nations in South America. Few Americans today remember the Malmedy massacre, for which forty-two former members of the Waffen SS—including Colonel Joachim Peiper, commander of the First SS Panzer Regiment, the core group involved in the slaughter—were sentenced to death by hanging. Even fewer Americans remember that, despite the convictions and death sentences given to these forty-two Nazis for killing more than eighty-four American POWs in cold blood on December 14, 1944, (the second day of fighting in the Battle of the Bulge) the sentences of all the Waffen SS convicted in the Malmedy Trial were commuted to life imprisonment—and all were released one by one, with Colonel Peiper being the last.

Hitler's escape began in 1943, when Martin Bormann implemented a plan to invest billions of dollars of stolen wealth in corporations with a particular focus on business enterprises in the United States and Argentina. The ties between Wall Street and the Hitler regime forged as Hitler was coming to power before World War II proved to be useful once again when Allen Dulles served the interests of the Roosevelt administration in Berne, Switzerland, for the duration of the war. With Bormann relying heavily upon Swiss banks and financial agents to effect his transactions, Dulles could anticipate a continuation of the pre-war alliances that had been forged between US companies and German companies. While the post-war Marshall Plan rebuilt German infrastructure, Dulles and Bormann quietly created a capital base for a post-war boom in the United States and a Germany destined to emerge as the economic powerhouse behind a united Europe put together through the early free trade compacts masterminded by French internationalist Jean Monnet.

Truthfully, Hitler could not have escaped without the complicity of Allen Dulles in Switzerland and Juan Perón. Having the world believe Hitler committed suicide rather than convicting and sentencing him to death during a war crimes tribunal avoided the creation of a Nazi martyr for future generations. Suicide, however, when seen as the final act of a coward, is hard to admire. In many ways, the dilemma Roosevelt, and then Truman, faced at the end of World War II was similar to the dilemma Abraham Lincoln faced at the end of the Civil War. "If you bring these [Confederate] leaders to trial, it will condemn the North, for by the Constitution, secession is not rebellion," Chief Justice Salmon P. Chase said in July 1867. "Lincoln wanted [Jefferson] Davis to escape, and he was right. His capture was a mistake. His trial will be a greater one."[175] Perón could quietly provide a safe haven for Hitler, knowing he would have to remain in hiding the rest of his life. The moment he resurfaced as a public figure or allowed the remaining Nazis to reform a national socialist movement with his backing, Hitler would have signed his death warrant. The history of the Nazis in South America is that they attempted to live out their lives in hiding, so as to enjoy freedom in their final years without having to face the consequences of being apprehended and brought to justice.

Today, a convincing argument can be made that the Fourth Reich is arising today in the United States and Europe. "At the beginning of the third millennium after Christ, by most criteria, the once-free constitutional republic of the United States had become a National Socialist nation, an empire of the creators of the Third Reich— a Fourth Reich," wrote journalist Jim Marrs in his 2008 book *The Rise of the Fourth Reich: The Secret Societies that Threaten to Take Over America*.[176] What Allen Dulles perceived was that the twentieth century was shaping into a conflict not between capitalism and communism, but between national socialism and communism. With the coming of the New Deal, both the established Republican and Democratic Parties bought into the idea that social welfare was the responsibility of an ever-expanding federal government. Since the 1930s, with rare exceptions,

---

[175] Chief Justice Salmon P. Chase, quoted in Shelby Foote, *The Civil War: Red River to Appomatix*, Vol. 3, (New York: Random House, 1974), p. 765.

[176] Jim Marrs, *The Rise of the Fourth Reich: The Secret Societies that Threaten to Take Over America* (New York: William Morrow, 2008), p. 5.

so-called "big-government Republicans" have dominated the establishment of the Republican Party.

In a real sense, we have become the modern-day national socialists, in that the United States political consensus assumes that the government's responsibility is both to provide the regulatory structure and economic stability for government to form a partnership with business, while taxing the people and the corporations to provide abundant social welfare support to sustain those struggling to achieve or maintain some level of middle-class stability. Seeing the fundamental agreement between the Nazi's National Socialist political philosophy and New Deal thinking, the precursor to today's progressive thinking, Allen Dulles knew the Nazis working for Hitler in government, business, and intelligence activities were our natural allies.

Dulles not only masterminded co-opting Reinhard Gehlen's Wehrmacht intelligence agency to craft the CIA, he also masterminded "Operation Paperclip" to bring thousands of German scientists, engineers, and otherwise technically skilled experts to the United States to work in the retooling of US business from their war-production orientation to the competence needed to dominate the post-war economy worldwide. Just as US intelligence operations at the end of World War II were based on the Nazis, JFK relied on Nazi rocket scientist and aerospace engineer Wernher von Braun to build the intercontinental ballistic missiles the United States would need in the atomic era and to create the NASA infrastructure, which would lead to the United States landing on the moon.

It is far from certain that the United States and Western Europe would have had the economic strength to withstand an expanding Soviet Union throughout the

Cold War years had Bormann not invested the ill-gotten Nazi capital—including the wealth stolen from the Jews about to be murdered—in the Western economies in order to establish viable escape routes for himself, Hitler, other top Nazis such as Heinrich Müller, and tens of thousands of other Nazi war criminals. Without Dulles's complicity, it is much less likely that Hitler or any of the other Nazi henchmen like Eichmann and Mengele would ever have escaped. Without Bormann's funding, it is much less certain that Ronald Reagan would have had the economic base from which to challenge Gorbachev to tear down the Berlin Wall.

When the Nazis escaped Germany at the end of World War II, they brought with them not only the advanced technical genius of Nazi science and capital derived from the conquest and slavery the Nazis imposed on Europe—they also brought their ideology with them. Ironically, the Nazis lost World War II, but through the economic deceit of free trade agreements, Hitler's dream of a united Europe ruled by Germany has been partially realized in today's European Union. Through the same route of deceitful trade agreements that formed the World Trade Organization and NAFTA, the United States has championed international organizations, beginning with the United Nations and continuing with the International Monetary Fund and the World Bank, that threaten to end US sovereignty once and for all. The Constitution for which tens of thousands of patriotic and brave men and women fought Germany in two twentieth century wars is being eroded today as internationalists of both the Republican and Democratic Parties look to enrich themselves in a global economy that favors Germany in the West and China in the East.

"America today is a national socialist's dream come true," Jim Marrs wrote.[177] As the National Security Agency engages in a program of universal domestic surveillance unimaginable even to the Nazis at the height of their power, American businesses have abandoned Detroit to go bankrupt as cars and trucks sold in the United States are manufactured via the mechanisms of a one-world economy. Meanwhile, those Americans who dare champion principles of US freedoms as traditionally defined by the US Constitution, the Declaration of Independence, and the Bill of Rights face ridicule and derision as "tea-baggers," instead of the Tea Party Patriots they truly are. Shockingly, the once proud US mainstream media has abandoned its role as the Fourth Estate to buy into the dominant government welfare state ideology with a willing compliance Hitler would never have thought possible. Just as Hitler was allowed to escape Berlin and permitted to enter Argentina by submarine, national socialism has thrived in what is arguably the Fourth Reich that we ourselves have unwittingly become.

---

[177] Ibid., p. 363.

INDEX